Organizations,
Clubs,
Action Groups

Organizations, Clubs, Action Groups:

How to Start Them, How to Run Them

ELSIE E. WOLFERS
and VIRGINIA B. EVANSEN

ST. MARTIN'S PRESS   New York

This book is dedicated to two internationally recognized women:

Florence Feiler, literary consultant and agent for the Ruhgstedlund Foundation of Denmark, and many others in countries around the world.

Dr. Margaret Hasebroock, Past President of the International General Federation of Woman's Clubs, The National Association of Parliamentarians, The National League of American PenWoman, Inc., Vice President and Dean of Education of Freedom's Foundation of Valley Forge, Pa., who has served on many international and national executive boards.

It is because of the encouragement and advice from these two outstanding women, that this book has been written.

Copyright © 1980 by Elsie E. Wolfers and Virginia B. Evansen
For information, write: St. Martin's Press,
175 Fifth Avenue, New York, N.Y. 10010
Manufactured in the United States of America

Library of Congress Cataloging in Publication Data
Wolfers, Elsie E
   Organizations, clubs, action groups.

   1. Clubs—Handbooks, manuals, etc. I. Evansen,
Virginia Besaw, joint author. II. Title.
HS2519.W64   367'.068   80-23198
ISBN 0-312-58791-0

Design by A. Christopher Simon

10 9 8 7 6 5 4 3 2 1

First Edition

Contents

v

Preface

Today consumers unite to fight inflation through co-op buying. Renters and home and condominium owners organize to protect contracts, enforce upkeep, and build recreational facilities. Volunteers join groups that assist in hospitals, raise funds for library equipment, and promote better nursing-home care for the elderly.

Membership groups with common interests also develop in the professional world of science and business. Thousands of associations exist for hobbyists and sports enthusiasts. More are being formed every day by ecologists and professional people in education and the creative arts.

What these organizations lack are detailed guidelines under which to operate. Many presidents have no clear knowledge of their duties; many secretaries do not know how to take minutes; and some treasurers cannot balance their own checkbooks.

In years of working in executive capacities with such groups as The National League of American Pen Women, The Federation of Women's Clubs, The Sunnyvale Friends of the Library, Children's Civic Theater, Teach, Fairbrae Swim and Tennis Club, opera and hospital auxiliaries and many others, we have found that clubs tend to flounder, not because of lack of willingness on the part of members, but because of lack of policy under which the officers and chairpersons should operate.

In this book we have set out the functions and responsibilities of officers and board members, broken down into simple steps which can be followed easily. Those wishing to form a group will find procedures for local, state, and national organization. We have also included outlines for planning national and state conventions, exhibitions, special events, and fund raising which can be adapted to the needs of different groups.

ELSIE E. WOLFERS
VIRGINIA B. EVANSEN

Chapter I

The Rewards and Responsibilities of Belonging to an Organization

People join organizations because of the benefits they will gain. While the answer to "What's in it for me" is the reason for joining, responsibilities as well as rewards come with the membership card. To gain the most benefit, members should be aware of their reasons for affiliating with the group and should shoulder their share of responsibility.

Responsibilities:

1. *Attend meetings.* "I don't know what's going on" is a complaint frequently heard. The chances are that member hasn't attended a meeting in six months.
2. *Be punctual.* The habitually late member disrupts the meeting and annoys others.
3. *Pay dues on time.* The treasurer who makes ten calls to remind a member to write a check is a jewel. Not too many of these exist. If you do not intend to renew your membership, you should send a letter of resignation. If you slide past the renewal date by two or

1

three months, you may find yourself dropped for nonpayment of dues. Reinstatement, especially in professional societies, can be difficult.

4. *Be supportive,* loyal, and enthusiastic.

5. *Question if you don't understand the discussion.* If you are floundering, the chances are other members are puzzled. Ask for an explanation. It is your right, and the rest of the membership will thank you for it.

6. *Speak out.* Many times a vocal minority runs an organization because the majority of members are afraid to open their mouths.

7. *Accept majority decisions.* It is your right to question and vote no, but, when the ayes have it, you should accept the decision gracefully. The member who threatens resignation when outvoted is a poor sport. You do have the right of resignation if the group embarks on a course that you cannot morally or ethically accept. However, if the group tackles a project that you think will be unprofitable, or elects an officer that you believe incapable, you should still give the organization your support and work to try to change the situation.

8. *Be prepared to complete any job you accept.* If you don't have the time, don't let yourself be talked into taking a position as a committee head. When you accept the responsibility of office, plan your activities so you can perform your duties efficiently and enthusiastically. If your health, family, or work situation changes, so that you can no longer function properly, notify the president at once. A secretary who resigns is better than a secretary who never attends a meeting.

9. *Be friendly to new members.* By making them welcome, you may gain lifelong friends.

10. *Keep your balance.* Don't live and breathe just for the Petunia Society. Don't let being a member become your only interest in life.

11. *Don't resign because you must be inactive.* While age or poor health may keep you from working on a committee, your support, through dues, is still valuable. An inactive member can still be a staunch advocate of the group. Many longtime members, because of loyalty and gratitude, make gifts to organizations or establish trust funds for its benefit.

Rewards:

1. *Meeting people and making friends.* Few of us are happy huddled in a cave, hermit-style. We want friends, and we need to meet people. What better way is there than by joining a group where shared interests provide common goals and enjoyment? Today's society is transient; 36 million Americans move each year. Joining an organization is an easy way to meet people in a new location. If you belong to a national association, you can transfer your membership and make instant acquaintances.

2. *The joy of accomplishment.* While most of us work for our bread and butter in mundane jobs, we taste the frosting of life by accomplishing something worthwhile. Raising money for scholarships, improving the community or environment, or striving to better conditions in nursing homes takes us out of the workday world and gives life more meaning.

3. *Widening your interests while having fun.* Organizations exist for almost everyone, from antique collectors to zoo supporters. Educational, hobby, cultural, and sports groups provide members the opportunity to write poetry, discuss Shakespeare, improve their painting or photography, grow better roses, visit museums, and fly kites—and have a good time while doing it.

4. *Developing qualities of leadership* and becoming known in the community. Many school-board and city-council members started their careers in a P.T.A. or home-owners association. The person who gets the shakes when faced with speaking before a group will gain self-assurance by working on or chairing a committee.

5. *Improving your finances.* Condominium and home-owners organize to protect members' financial investments. Co-op buying through an organization can help your food bill. Other groups offer members opportunities to buy equipment, insurance, or to travel at reduced rates.

6. *Opportunities for gaining well-rounded experience.* The man who spends his life in a single-project research lab can widen his horizons by directing a fund-raising drive. The woman who has been

busy with child care and the house will find that organizational work can supply experience and training and develop leadership qualities that will be valuable for reentry into the labor market. Today's personnel managers look for the well-rounded person. Experience and self-confidence gained in volunteer work is an asset.

8. *The intangibles.* While prestige, political, professional, or economic advantage, educational, cultural, and social opportunities can be the motives for joining an organization, the intangible rewards are the reasons most members continue to pay dues. When people unite to work for common interests, the "What's in it for me" changes to "What can I do to help," resulting in personal growth and expanded horizons. The respect, admiration, and close-knit relationships that develop among members cannot be measured.

Chapter II

Getting Organized

Your group may start with one person who wants to meet others to share ideas or work together on projects, creative endeavors, or hobbies. Before forming an organization, it is wise to investigate whether there is already in existence a similar group with the same objectives, either locally or nationally. Rather than start another organization, which duplicates effort and makes obtaining members and raising funds difficult, it might be wiser to join an existing group.

If you cannot find an organization that meets your needs, don't hesitate to start one. Faced with the failure of a developer to build a promised swimming pool and clubhouse, and the prospect of undesirable commercial zoning adjacent to their homes, three of the residents of a Sunnyvale, California, housing development did just that. They sent out a flyer inviting all of the home owners in the tract to a meeting to discuss the problems. From that meeting came a swim and tennis club with a membership of over 200 families and a home-owners' association that successfully protested the rezoning.

Forming an organization is not difficult. The formula for success is careful preplanning and a few people willing to do some work.

Preplanning: Although one person can work miracles, it is best to have five or seven involved in the planning.

5

1. Select a temporary secretary to take the minutes (see sample in Chapter V) of the planning sessions and the first meeting.

2. Choose a temporary presiding officer.

3. Prepare a statement of purpose for the organization. For example: "This organization shall promote literary and educational work of a professional nature."

4. Select a working name for the organization.

5. Get information on incorporation and tax exemption to present at the first meeting, if applicable. (See Chapters IX and X.)

6. Prepare tentative bylaws in advance to be presented for approval at the first meeting. (See "Bylaws and How to Write Them," Chapter III.)

7. Choose a place and date for the first meeting. You may choose someone's home or, if you hope to attract a large number of people, a meeting room in a church, school, bank, library, community center, or other public facility. In some areas, you will have to pay for the use of the room. In others, free meeting rooms are available. Some community-owned facilities prohibit political use or stipulate that all meetings must be open to the public. If your group will have a closed membership or a political purpose, you should check for such prohibition. Try to find a place with good parking facilities in a well-lighted area, especially if you are scheduling a night meeting. Make the reservation early. In some places, you will find meeting rooms booked a year or more in advance.

8. If a large attendance is anticipated, you should provide a podium and loud-speaker system for use by the chairperson and speakers.

9. Set the time most convenient for the membership you hope to attract. Remember that over 50 percent of women today are in the work force and will be unable to attend morning or afternoon meetings. If your group will be composed of retired persons, a daytime meeting will be best. If people of all ages are among your prospective membership, a 7:30 to 9:30 P.M. meeting can be a good hour. However, you should consider that many women do not like to go out alone at night.

10. Make arrangements to notify the prospective members of the

meeting. An advertisement in your local paper or a notice in the classified section can help inform people about the meeting. The formation of an organization with the purpose of community improvement or enrichment can be newsworthy. Notify the editor of your local paper of the location, day, and time of the meeting, and include an invitation to send a reporter. Distribute a flyer setting forth the time, date, place, and purpose of the meeting to possible members.

The Organizational Meeting:

1. The meeting can open with a ten-minute period for people to introduce themselves and get acquainted.

2. The presiding officer calls the meeting to order immediately following this.

3. Approval of the persons serving as temporary presiding officer and secretary must be made by those present.

4. The secretary sends around an attendance sheet with space for names, addresses, and telephone numbers.

5. The presiding officer calls upon the person responsible for the meeting to explain why this group should organize formally. The proposed objectives and activities should be given clearly and simply. The presiding officer then asks for discussion. When organizing, it is best to allow informal discussion of objectives and bylaws.

6. If, after discussion of the purposes and activities, the group decides to organize, the tentative bylaws are presented for discussion and approval.

7. The nominating committee should be appointed at this time as outlined in the bylaws.

8. If the group decides incorporation is desirable, a committee is appointed to further investigate the procedure.

9. The time, place, and date of the following meeting is set. If the objectives of the organization require action within a short time, this meeting may be held within a week. The temporary presiding officer announces that dues will be collected and officers elected at this meeting.

The Second Meeting:

1. The temporary presiding officer calls the meeting to order.

2. The secretary reads the minutes.

3. The presiding officer asks for the report of the nominating committee. (See "Duties of Committee Chairpersons," Chapter VI.)

4. Officers are elected as prescribed in the bylaws.

5. The newly elected president takes charge of the meeting.

6. The president calls upon the treasurer, who announces that dues are payable. The treasurer should be prepared to write receipts, keeping a carbon with names and addresses.

7. The president reminds the members of the objectives of the group and asks for discussion. After a reasonable length of time, the president brings the discussion to a close and asks for a motion regarding the activities to take place. This action may be an immediate step, if the group has formed to protest zoning, enforce a contract, or engage in such activities as co-op buying. Other organizations may wish to proceed in a more leisurely manner, through the appointment of study committees.

Chapter III

Bylaws and How to Write Them

Bylaws are the rules that define the duties, responsibilities, and privileges of the officers and members. They guide the organization in carrying out the purposes for which it was formed. Bylaws are so named because they are not the laws of the country. They do not affect everybody, but only those people who belong to, or work in, the organization that has made the bylaws. During the preplanning session, a committee of three should be chosen to write a set of tentative bylaws to be presented at the first meeting.

Essentials of Good Bylaws:

1. Bylaws should be written in simple language, using as few words as possible, yet clearly describing the meaning of each rule.

2. A bylaw should never be written that serves to act against the law.

3. Avoid badly written bylaws. For example: "Bylaws may be amended by an affirmative vote of two-thirds of the members" is a poor bylaw. So many votes might be hard to obtain, especially in a large organization. The bylaw should read "Bylaws may be amended by an affirmative vote of two-thirds of the members *present.*"

4. Essentials for conducting the business of the organization must not be overlooked.

5. Discussion should never be prohibited by bylaws. Time limitations must be put into the rules of order.

MODEL BYLAWS

The following bylaws are presented as a suggested form that can be adapted to the needs of individual organizations. Discussion, in parenthesis, follows each section.

BYLAWS
of

NAME OF ORGANIZATION ....

HEADQUARTERS ADDRESS ....

ARTICLE 1—NAME

The name of this organization shall be ....
(See "Incorporation," Chapter IX. While you may not plan to incorporate, a distinctive name that describes your organization is an asset. To avoid confusion in the mails and in fund-raising and other activities, it is wise to choose a name that is not identical or similar to that of an existing group.)

ARTICLE 2—PURPOSES

The purposes of this organization are:
1. To promote the development of ....
2. To assist members to achieve ....
3. To make scholarships available to ....
(If the organization is interested in being eligible for tax-exempt status from the Internal Revenue Service, please read "Incorporation," Chapter IX and "Taxes," Chapter X.)

ARTICLE 3—MEMBERSHIP

Section 1.   Types of membership shall consist of active, associate, life, and honorary memberships.

        A.   Active membership requires that the member be ....

B.   Associate membership shall have the same requirements and privileges as active members,
excepting that associate members may not vote
or hold office.

C.   Life membership is offered to those members
who donate . . . . . . to the organization.

D.   Honorary membership may be conferred upon
an individual provided . . . . and is
chosen by the executive board for such honor.
Such a member is entitled to the same privileges
as an active member.

*(Although there may be many categories of members, the commit-
tee need choose only those which best suit the organization's
needs.)*

Section 2.   Qualifications for admittance to this organization are

. . . .

*(An organization may have special qualifications for membership,
such as occupation, residence within certain geographical areas, or
specified professional standards. According to law, an applicant
for membership in a nonprofit, tax-exempt organization may not
be disqualified because of sex or race.)*

Section 3.   Application for membership must be sponsored by
two members of the organization, in good standing.

(Any organization open to the public must accept all applicants.)

Section 4.   Initiation Fees and Dues.

A.   Initiation fees shall be . . . . . . and included with
the application. Annual dues must also be included at the same time.

*(You may not need initiation fees. However, the fee helps cover
the expense of application forms, brochures, and membership
certificates.)*

B.   Annual dues shall be . . . . . , payable to the
treasurer not later than . . . . each year.

*(Your organization may wish to establish varied dues for special
categories of membership, such as lowered fees for students or
persons over sixty-five years. Museum-support and other such*

groups may offer patron, sustaining, and contributing member-
ships at higher dues. In some professional organizations, associate
members who have not yet fully qualified for active membership
pay lower dues.)

Section 5.   Resignation and Renewal of Membership

       A.   A member who resigns in good standing (dues
           paid up to date) may reapply for membership
           within the period of . . . .

       B.   Reinstatement requires a fee of . . . .

Section 6.   Dropped from Membership for Nonpayment of Dues

       A.   A member who has not paid the current dues by
           . . . . will be dropped from membership
           after notification by mail from the treasurer.

       B.   A member who has been dropped may reinstate
           membership by payment of all dues in arrears
           and a reinstatement fee of . . . .

(Members who resign or are dropped may have to requalify when
the bylaws require it.)

ARTICLE 4—THE EXECUTIVE BOARD

Section 1.   The board shall consist of the elected officers and the
           appointed committee heads.

(We believe that all committee heads, except for those appointed
for a short period of time for a special study, should be members of
the board. Special and study committees can be handled in the
rules of order.)

Section 2.   The executive board shall handle the regular business
           of the organization.

(Business of the organization should never be placed in the hands
of the entire membership. This entails much unnecessary discus-
sion and loss of time, which could otherwise be spent in pursuing
the objectives of the organization. If the organization is small and
meets regularily, the board may submit recommendations to the
membership for approval.)

Section 3.   Meetings. Regular meetings of the executive board
           shall be held . . . .

(Monthly or whatever the bylaws committee recommends.)

Section 4.   Quorem. A quorem for conducting the business of the executive board shall be not less than . . . . . . members of the board empowered to vote.

(Heads of special and study committees appointed for a short period of time do not have a vote. This should be a part of standing rules.)

Section 5.   Each outgoing board must leave in the treasury a sum equal to the unpaid bills or obligations for which the administration is responsible.

(It is desirable to leave funds so that the next administration begins with a favorable balance. This can be part of standing rules.)

ARTICLE 5—OFFICERS AND COMMITTEE CHAIRPERSONS

Section 1.   There shall be the following elected officers.
   A.   President
   B.   Vice-president or vice-presidents
   C.   Recording secretary
   D.   Corresponding secretary
   E.   Treasurer

(A large organization may desire to have two, three, four or more vice-presidents to carry out different activities. The duties of the corresponding and recording secretaries may be combined. The organization may elect other officers, such as an assistant treasurer, if it so desires.)

Section 2.   An officer who does not comply with assigned responsibilities may be relieved of office by majority vote of the executive board. Appointment of a replacement shall be made by the president with the approval of the board.

Section 3.   The heads of committees shall be appointed by the president immediately after installation. They are approved by the elected board.

(They may be membership, public relations, hospitality, etc., or any permanent committee needed to carry out the purposes of the organization.)

ARTICLE 6—ELECTIONS

Section 1.

    A.   Nominations: A nominating committee consisting of a chairperson and two members shall be elected at the time of regular elections. At the end of the term, their duty is to nominate the officers and nominating committee for the next administration.

(The nominating committee may be appointed by the president or elected by the membership two or three months before election. We recommend election of the committee a year in advance, because this removes the danger that the president may appoint personal friends to control nominations. It also gives the committee a year to consider which members are most qualified for office.)

    B.   Report of the nominating committee shall be made at the (date) . . . . meeting.

    C.   Nominations from the floor will be in order at the . . . . meeting.

Section 2.

    A.   An elections committee of three members shall be appointed by the president to conduct the elections according to the procedures set up in the standing rules.

    B.   Election shall be by secret ballot.

(Some organizations, particularly small ones, may vote by a show of hands or a vocal aye or nay. It is wise, however, even in a small group to vote by ballot. This avoids hurt feelings and mistaken count.)

    C.   Voting privileges.

(Usually each member has one vote, but organizations with different categories of membership will have to establish varied voting privileges. For example, a home-owners' association with family members may limit voting rights to one vote per family. In professional groups, associate members have no vote.)

Section 3.

    A.   Term of Office. Officers shall be elected for a term of . . . . . . year(s), to serve from the time of installation in . . . . . . until the succeeding installation of officers in . . . . . .

(It is essential that the bylaws state exactly when a term of office starts and when it ends.)

    B.   Officers may not serve more than . . . . . . years. There must be an interval of at least . . . . . . administrations between each term.

(Officers should not succeed themselves indefinitely, because this can create stagnation in an organization. Most officers serve for a period of one to two years. Some groups allow a second term, but usually this must be served after an interval of one or two administrations.)

Section 4.   Transition of Administration: There shall be a meeting of the executive boards immediately following installation. It should include the outgoing and incoming officers and the committee chairpersons. Upon the introduction of new business, the gavel, charter, and files are turned over to the newly installed president, who then becomes the presiding officer.

(Transition from one administration to the next should be given some consideration in setting up the bylaws. Although the new officers have been installed, the outgoing administration will still have some old business, such as final expenditures of the elections committee, to complete at the combined board meeting. Once this is concluded, the new president continues the meeting with only the new board present. The past president can be asked to serve in an advisory capacity.)

ARTICLE 7—DUTIES OF OFFICERS

Section 1.   The president shall

    A.   preside at all meetings of the executive board

and general meetings of the organization, and at any special meetings;

B.   appoint the committee heads immediately after installation;

C.   make interim appointments as needed with the approval of the executive board;

D.   sign all checks with the treasurer;

E.   sign all contracts with the recording secretary after approval of the executive board;

F.   sign all membership cards with the treasurer;

G.   serve as an ex-officio member of all committees except that of the nominating committee; and

H.   call a special meeting when it is necessary.

(It is not necessary to spell out all the duties of the president in the bylaws. See "Duties of the President," Chapter IV.)

Section 2.   The vice-president shall perform the duties of an absent president and perform such duties as are assigned by the president.

(Customarily the vice-president is asked to serve as program chairperson. If the organization has several vice-presidents, they are assigned duties by the president.)

Section 3.   The recording secretary shall record the minutes of all proceedings of the board and membership meetings and, with the president, shall sign all contracts for the organization.

Section 4.   The corresponding secretary shall handle the correspondence of the organization.

Section 5.   The treasurer shall

A.   have charge of all the funds of the organization;

B.   make an (annual, quarterly) . . . . financial report to the membership;

C.   sign all checks with the president;

D.   sign all membership cards with the president;

E.   keep dues collected in advance for the next administration in a separate fund;

F.   be bonded; and

       G.   keep restricted funds of the organization in separate accounts.

(It is only necessary to bond the treasurer when large sums of money are involved. See "Duties of the Other Officers," Chapter V; "Finances," Chapter XI.)

ARTICLE 8—MEETINGS

Section 1.   There shall be an (annual, semiannual, quarterly) meeting during the months of . . . . Notice of such meeting shall be given each member at least . . . . . . days before the meeting.

Section 2.   Special meetings may be called by the president or the board. Upon written notice of . . . . . . members, the president shall call a meeting. Notice of special meetings shall be given to the members at least . . . . . . days in advance.

Section 3.   A quorem for conducting business of a regular or special meeting of the membership shall be not less than . . . . . . members empowered to vote.

(What percentage of the membership constitutes a quorem should be decided by the committee. In formal legislative meetings, it may be a majority. In informal social or professional groups, it may be as little as one-quarter of the membership.)

ARTICLE 9—RESTRICTED FUNDS

Section 1.   Scholarship funds must be used as designated by the donor.

Section 2.   Endowments and Restricted Funds: Only the interest earned by endowments and restricted funds may be used for the designated purpose of each fund.

ARTICLE 10—DISCIPLINE

Section 1.   Charges of professional dishonesty, working against the principles and purposes of the organization, and/or injuring the professional standing of a member, may be filed in a written statement signed by five members in good standing and sent to the executive board.

Section 2.   The accused member shall be notified in writing of the action and shall have the privilege of being present at a special or regular meeting of the executive board, at which the charges will be considered.

Section 3.   The member may be suspended by a two-thirds vote or expelled by a three-fourths vote of the executive board.

(Discipline should be included in the bylaws, to avoid problems within the membership. Organizations must recognize that dishonest or unscrupulous persons may join and must be prepared to handle the situation. It is recommended that the executive board appoint a committee to investigate the charges and make a report. The board can then make the proper decision regarding appropriate discipline. A guilty member should be asked to resign rather than face expulsion. The situation is kept confidential.)

Article 11—Amendments

The bylaws may be amended or revised by an affirmative vote of two-thirds (or as determined) of all the members present at a meeting designed for that purpose. Copies of proposed amendments shall be given members in writing at least . . . . months prior to the meeting.

(Because bylaws may only be amended or revised, it is desirable to keep them flexible, by outlining the duties of the officers and executive board. Detailed instructions can be provided in job descriptions. These can be changed by a majority vote of the membership or executive board.

Amendments usually require the submission of the proposed amendment to the parliamentarian for study before the amendment can be presented to the executive board for approval. The membership then must be notified what amendment or amendments are to be voted upon, at a stated meeting at least two months before the meeting takes place.

Two-thirds of the members present must approve the amendment. It is then officially included in the bylaws, which will have to be reprinted. Since all of this is time consuming, it can easily hamper the business of the organization. It is therefore important that the committee write good bylaws that do not need to be amended frequently.

A committee of three, appointed by the president and approved by the executive board, should review and evaluate bylaws every five years, or as necessary. Bylaws should not be considered a rigid instrument that can never be changed. Organizations can outgrow their original bylaws, and revision may be necessary.)

ARTICLE 12—DISSOLUTION *(Alternate)*

Should the organization be dissolved, all material possessions of the organization must be sold and the monies obtained from the sale divided equally between all members after all bills have been paid.

(This form may be used by an organization which is not a nonprofit corporation or has not obtained tax-exempt status from the Internal Revenue Service.)

ARTICLE 12—DISSOLUTION *(Alternate)*

In the event of dissolution of . . . . , remaining assets after the satisfaction of all obligations of the corporation shall be distributed for purposes within the scope of Internal Revenue Service Code 501(c)(3), or amendments thereof.

(This form must be followed by a nonprofit tax-exempt corporation. Nonprofit associations should follow a similar form providing that the assets be given to another like organization. In some cases, the state may take upon itself the task of handling such a dissolution.)

RULES OF ORDER

Many organizations use *Roberts' Rules of Order, Newly Revised,* as a parliamentary authority. While such procedure may be necessary in large meetings, we feel that organizations will benefit by developing their own rules of order, to avoid the limitations of putting motions before debate.

We recommend that members attempt to reach agreement regarding proposed activities through discussion, before a motion is made. After such agreement has been reached, the president may ask for a motion. It is made and passed, so that there is record of the action in the minutes book. For example: an organization may have a surplus of $200, which members wish to donate for a charitable purpose. After general discussion of three possible projects, they decide to buy a sixteen-millimeter projector for a senior citizens' center. Then a member says, "I move that we spend $200 to buy a sixteen-millimeter projector for the senior citizens' center." The president repeats the motion and asks for a vote. Approval is given by a majority of the members present.

Many organizations use this informal way of handling business, even though their bylaws give *Roberts' Rules* as the parliamentary authority. Through experience they have found that the discussion is more amenable, and they prefer to avoid the heated debate that can follow a motion. For this method to work, the president has to keep the discussion centered on the agenda item.

Election to the office of president should not deprive that individual of the right and privilege of discussion. Frequently the president may be the most knowledgeable member of the organization regarding a proposal before the membership and should enter into the debate. Although the formality of "Vacating the Chair" is a tradition, it is not necessary to follow this time-wasting procedure.

We believe that organizations can operate efficiently by using five essential motions:

1. *Motion for Action.* A proposal by a member that the organization do a specified thing. Example: "I move that we hold a rummage sale to raise money for our scholarship fund."

2. *Motion to Amend.* Amendment of a motion may be made by insertion, addition, deletion, or substitution. Example: "I move to amend the motion by insertion of the words 'in May' after the word 'sale.'" This much of an amendment can be handled easily. It is better to ask that the original motion be withdrawn and a new one substituted if several changes are proposed.

3. *Motion to Rescind.* Once a motion has been approved, reflection or investigation may prove it to be impractical. Because the motion is in the minutes book, it must be repealed before a different course of action is decided. Example: "I move that the motion that we have a rummage sale to raise money for our scholarship fund be rescinded." To avoid rescinding motions, we recommend discussion and investigation where necessary before action is taken.

4. *Motion to Table.* This cuts off discussion and action on a motion that has been made. When an organization arrives at agreement before a motion is made, it is rarely needed. However, a motion to table allows time for further investigation and ends heated discussion. This motion must be voted upon at once. Example: "I move that we table the motion that we hold a rummage sale to raise money for the scholarship fund." Approval of a motion to table does not mean that the original motion is defeated. After investigation, it may be brought back at a future meeting.

5. *Motion to Suspend the Order of Business.* This is made when circumstances such as an interruption, late arrival, or early departure necessitate an alteration or change in the agenda. Example: "I move that we suspend the order of business to discuss fund-raising immediately after the minutes are read."

Proper Ways of Making Motions:

1. The person making the motion should provide the recording secretary with a written copy.

2. Motions should be written in short, clear sentences, so they cannot be misinterpreted.

3. A motion that is not relevant to the discussion is out of order.

4. Although it is customary in order to prevent frivolous motions, which only take up time, it is not essential that motions be seconded.

SAMPLE RULES OF ORDER

1. Discussion on any one agenda item shall be limited to . . . . . . minutes.

2. A member may not speak more than twice for or against any agenda item.

3. Members may be asked not to speak longer than two minutes each during discussion.

4. Members should not prolong discussion by repeating an argument already made by another member.

5. The order of business belongs in the rules of order.

STANDING RULES

Standing rules are an expansion of the bylaws, detailing the rights, privileges, and limitations of members. They are designed to take care of the business of the organization in a practical manner. They may be necessary to the health and safety of the members. For example: the time a meeting should start and where it will take place belong in standing rules. These rules can be easily changed when necessary by a majority vote of the members present.

Sample Standing Rules

1. Meetings must be adjourned by 10 P.M.

2. Family members under 15 years may not bring guests into the club without written permission of a parent.

3. Name tags must be worn at all meetings.

4. Committee members working on an event pay the same admission as other members.

5. Running is not allowed on the pool deck.

Chapter IV

Duties of the President

The president and other officers take office for the first time at an installation ceremony, which may be as simple or as elaborate as the membership likes. At installation, the gavel and, if the organization has such insignia, a president's pin are presented to the incoming president. The new president may then give a short speech outlining goals and plans for the administration.

Once the excitement of election and the installation ceremony are over, the new president is faced with the duty and responsibility of seeing that the organization continues to function smoothly. "What do I do? Where do I go for help? How do I start?" are questions frequently asked, especially if the organization is new or has found it necessary to elect a relatively inexperienced member to office.

We recommend that the incoming president study the organization's charter or articles of incorporation, and its bylaws, rules of order, and standing rules. The files and reports should be turned over to the new president as soon as possible after election. They should be reviewed with the outgoing president, and any problem areas that might affect the office should be discussed.

At the organization's meetings, the president has the following duties:

23

Presiding: The president presides at all meetings. The vice-president must be informed in ample time if the president cannot attend. The agenda and all necessary materials must be made available for the meeting.

Agenda: The president sets up the agenda, so the corresponding secretary can provide a copy for each member of the board one week before the meeting. The agenda includes the time, place, date, purpose, and business items, which are usually taken up in the following order of business:

1. Call to order.
2. Pledge of Allegiance.
3. An inspirational message of nonsectarian character that will not offend any segment of the membership.
4. Roll call, or an attendance sheet may be passed and then recorded in the minutes.
5. Introduction of guests.
6. Announcements. Many organizations leave announcements for last. We believe they should be made early in the meeting before members start to leave.
7. Reading of minutes of the previous meeting by the recording secretary. The president asks for additions or corrections and, finally, approval. On approval, the president and the recording secretary initial and date the minutes.
8. Reports of officers in proper order: vice-president, corresponding secretary, treasurer. The financial statement is filed with the recording secretary.
9. Committee reports.
10. Reports of study or special committees.
11. Unfinished business. Business previously discussed without action may be reopened at this time.
12. Correspondence read by the corresponding secretary. Action related to correspondence takes place during new business. Reading correspondence at this time facilitates handling items which are new business.
13. New business.

14. Program. The meeting is usually turned over to the program chairperson who introduces the speaker.

15. Adjournment.

Visitors: Usually visitors are not invited to meetings. Speakers should not be expected to sit through the business, which should be handled before or after the program. National and state officers who attend a local meeting are introduced to the members and seated to the right of the president. They are invited to speak at an appropriate time.

In addition, the president has the following responsibilities:

Appointments:

1. Before election, the nominee for president should consider the qualifications of members to be appointed to the executive board.

2. With the approval of the elected officers, the president appoints the committee chairpersons. If a large yearly function or fund-raising affair will be a club activity, a committee should be appointed well in advance. A feasibility study of the function with committee recommendations should be submitted at the first executive board meeting. Many groups appoint two people to share a position requiring much work and detailed planning.

3. Special or study committees are appointed as needed. They cease to function as soon as the duty for which they were appointed is completed.

4. The parliamentarian is appointed by the president.

Contracts: All contracts must be signed by both the president and the recording secretary.

Checks: Both the president and the treasurer must sign all checks.

Voting: The president votes to break a tie. The president has a vote when voting is done by ballot.

Public Relations: Shortly after taking office, the president meets with the people in charge of public relations, membership, programs, and the newsletter, to plan a good publicity campaign.

Installation of New Administration: The president turns the files over to the incoming president and serves in an advisory capacity thereafter only when asked.

HOW TO BE A GOOD PRESIDENT

Qualities: The ideal president is a person with tact, ability to get along with people, a businesslike approach, cordial manner, patience, and time to spend on the business of the organization. With the responsibility and honor of the office goes the task of running the organization along lines that will keep the members interested and happy.

Background: A complete knowledge of the group's background is essential if the president is to operate efficiently. Upon election the president should review the bylaws and read the reports and minutes of the past several years.

Transition: A meeting with the outgoing president to discuss the past year's activities and the organization's goals or purpose will make the transition easier.

Best Use of the Vice-President: The president should keep the vice-president up-to-date on the concerns of the organization. For example: there might be a question of unethical behavior by a member, which would merit expulsion. Until the discipline committee completes its investigation, the situation would be kept confidential. The vice-president should be informed, because this officer would have to take charge if the president suddenly became incapacitated.

Purpose: The president should always keep the group's purpose in mind. At times a member with a pet charity or political leaning may attempt to get the club's support. If it does not tie in with the purpose of the club, the activity should be discouraged.

Starting Time: The president should call the meeting to order on time. To delay the start of a meeting for members who are habitually tardy is to insult those who make an effort to be on time.

Tardiness: If many members are habitually late, a reexamination of the starting time might be in order. Some groups serve coffee and tea for a fifteen minute period before the meeting. This hospitality time gives the members a chance to talk with one another, ask questions of chairpersons or the president, and take care of minor details of business.

Presiding: As presiding officer, it is the responsibility of the president to keep the business meeting running smoothly. Committee heads should be asked to make their reports clear and concise.

Discussion: The president must handle discussions with tact, cordiality, and firmness. In a formal meeting, it is easy to do this by adhering to the rules of order.

It is in the informal meeting with controversial business that discussion is apt to be prolonged interminably. If this happens, the president should limit debate by asking each member to speak only twice. It may be necessary to request that personalities be avoided. When the group is evenly divided, it is best to suggest that the business be postponed and a committee appointed to investigate before action is taken.

Dealing with New Members: The president has to walk a fine line between the older member (both in years and length of membership) and the newer or younger member who wants to try a new approach to a project or suggests a different method of fund-raising.

The traditionalist objects with, "We've always done it this way." If this attitude is allowed to prevail, younger members may lose interest. Their response can be, "If you're going to continue to do it that way, do it yourself."

Behind the older member's objection can be fear of being left out or genuine concern that trouble will result. Since the traditionalist is usually sincerely and actively supportive of the organization, it is important that the president channel this energy into constructive effort.

One way of dealing with such situations is to ask this person to cochair the project with the newer member. The president has to handle the affair carefully, so that there is no danger of sabotage to prove that the old way is better.

Sometimes new members come on too strong. The organization is doing nothing right, and everything was done better in groups that they belonged to previously. This was the case with two P.T.A. members in Chicago. Immigrants from England, they extolled British schools, British methods, and British manners until the other members fervently, though silently, wished the family would return to its native land.

The president had a private talk with the Britishers, pointing out gently that their behavior was alienating members. Then the president asked them to prepare a program on the differences between British and American schools that would emphasize the best qualities of both systems.

Their informative speech delighted the other members. Best of all, preparing it provided the British pair with insight and knowledge of our school system, and they ceased to compare it constantly with that of England.

Membership: Most groups have increased membership as one goal. If membership remains static, organizations begin to decline. Members move, become ill, die, lose interest, take jobs that prevent them from being active, or, for other reasons, may not continue. Once membership decreases, obtaining new members becomes increasingly difficult. The exodus may snowball because the few remaining members become overworked and develop a "what's the use" attitude.

For these reasons, a continuing program to attract new members should be worked out with the membership chairperson. Steady growth can be expected when an organization offers a worthwhile purpose and participation in stimulating programs.

The president has the responsibility to welcome new members and introduce them. It is nice to appoint new people to committees in which they are interested, but new members should not be over-burdened with work of the organization. If this happens, they are apt to lose interest.

Troublemakers: Insecure people sometimes become troublemakers. If these people are given jobs that allow them to use their talents in productive ways, they can be turned into valuable members. The president must make a point of recognizing their contributions with public praise.

Discipline: For organizations of artists, photographers, writers, scientists, and other professionals to function properly, there must be ethical conduct on the part of members. Plagiarism and idea-stealing are considered heinous crimes by writers. Artists and photographers will not condone the copying of a picture with the attempt to pass it off as an original. Changing the position of a rose can ruin an exhibit at the fair.

Discipline procedure is written into the bylaws, outlining the method to be followed if a member willfully harms the group or another member. If charges are brought against a member, the president appoints a committee to investigate and report to the executive board. Every effort should be made to appoint impartial people who will keep the best interests of both the accused member and the organization in mind. (See "Bylaws and How to Write Them," Chapter III.)

Goals: For an organization to progress, the new president should have some goals in mind. For a home-owners' group, it may be a survey of proposed zoning changes. For a garden club, it can be the development of plants to win prizes. For a community improvement association, it may be the financing of a new park. The purpose of the organization and the abilities of the members should be considered when planning the year's goals and program.

Chapter V

Duties of Other Officers

While the president is the head of the organization, he or she can't function effectively without the support of the other officers. In order to carry out their responsibilities properly, it is essential that all newly elected officers review the charter or the articles of incorporation, the bylaws, the rules of order, and the standing rules. They should go over the files and reports with their predecessors and should keep careful records. At the end of the year, the files and a report should be turned over to the members of the next administration.

The duties of officers will, of course, vary in different organizations. However, the methods, procedures, and suggestions made in this chapter will help officers to function effectively.

THE VICE-PRESIDENT

Election to the office of vice-president is an honor and a mark of the membership's trust and respect. In the absence of the president, it is the vice-president's duty to conduct the business of the organization. Because this is a great responsibility, the president must keep the vice-president informed about the activities of the group, especially about any pending business that has not yet come before the executive board.

Presiding: When the president cannot attend, the vice-president presides at meetings.

Programs: Appointment of the vice-president to serve as program chairperson is customary in many organizations. The duties of the chairperson provide an excellent opportunity to demonstrate presidential qualifications, such as leadership and organizational management. However, it is the privilege of the president to ask the vice-president to serve in some other capacity in which the abilities of the officer can be better used.

Programs are a vital activity and have three main purposes:

1. To increase interest in the work of the organization.

2. To provide a variety of ideas to further the organization's purposes. In this way the work of the organization is promoted and interest kept alive.

3. To motivate members and guests to participate in the objectives of the group and to make financial contributions.

Presentation of Proposed Programs: As soon as possible after election, the program chairperson should present an outline of possible programs for the year to the executive board. The proposal should take into consideration the aims and objectives of the organization and the interests of its members. To avoid duplication, previous chairpersons should be consulted and past programs reviewed.

Budget: For the projected programs, a budget should be submitted to the budget chairperson in advance of the executive board meeting, so that the board can approve the programs and funds for them.

Program-Planning: The type of program will vary with each kind of organization. Naturally, the duties of the chairperson will also be somewhat different, but there are a few basic rules that will apply most of the time.

1. *Programs with Membership Participation:* The program chairperson should consult the Skills Inventory Cards (see "Duties of Committee Chairpersons," Chapter VI) to find out which members can provide interesting programs. Far too many organizations neglect talented members and always go outside the group for speakers. Use of members, when possible, stimulates their interest and helps to involve them further in the work of the organization. Members with specialized talents or abilities can be asked to give demonstrations. Exhibits of members' work can be an inspiration to others. Workshops conducted by members can be a means of gaining increased membership when guests are invited to attend.

2. *Arrangements for Programs With Outside Speakers:* The invitation to the speaker should be made three to four months in advance of the program. If the speaker is in great demand, arrangements may have to be made a year or more ahead of time. Be sure to have a "back up" program available, in case of last minute disappointment.

3. *Subject of the Speech:* This should be discussed in detail, so that the speaker understands the interests of the group and the length of time that will be allowed. The speaker should be informed if some particular emphasis is desired. A brochure in which the purposes of the organization are described will give the speaker an idea of how to slant the talk.

4. *Compensation:* A speaker who must travel a distance should be offered traveling expense and, if necessary, housing or payment for the cost of accommodations and extra meals. A complimentary meal should be offered if the speaker will be giving a talk following a luncheon or dinner. Depending on the funds made available by the budget, the speaker should be paid a reasonable honorarium or fee.

5. *Special Equipment:* Be sure to ask the speaker if any special equipment will be needed other than the usual microphone. List the items on your calendar so that you will have them in place before the meeting starts. The equipment should be checked out prior to the meeting to be certain that it is complete and in working condition. A pitcher of water and a glass should be provided and also an agenda or program.

6. *Publicity:* (See "Public Relations," Chapter XIV.) In order that

both the speaker and the program receive the necessary publicity to attract a good-sized audience, the program chairperson should confer with the public relations chairperson well in advance of the meeting date. The type of publicity desirable and what the program chairperson can do to further it should be discussed. The speaker should be asked to send a short biographical sketch and a black-and-white photograph with glossy finish and good contrast at least six weeks before the scheduled talk. The public relations chairperson must be provided with the speaker's full name (and title where it applies), photocopy of the biographical sketch, details of the complete program and objectives, title of speech, and date, time, and place where the program will be held.

7. *Verification with the Speaker:* A letter should be sent to the speaker listing all details relating to the presentation including date, time, topic, equipment, housing (if applicable), and fee. It should also request an affirmative reply that verifies the facts mentioned. This agreement becomes what in essence is a contract to complete the assignment. (See "Contracts, Insurance, and Permits," Chapter XII.)

8. *Reminder:* Check with the speaker a week or ten days ahead of time (especially if arrangements have been made months in advance), to be certain that nothing will interfere with the scheduled program.

9. *Arrival of Speaker:* If the speaker is coming from out of the area, arrange to meet at a specific place, such as the information booth or baggage exit. The speaker should be provided with a way of identifying the chairperson. Holding up the organization's brochure or a sign is a good idea. The speaker who comes directly to the meeting place is greeted at the door by the program chairperson, escorted to the head table, and introduced to the president. Normally, the guest speaker is seated to the right of the presiding officer.

10. *Introduction of Speaker:* The program chairperson introduces the speaker at the appropriate time, using the material supplied in the biographical sketch.

11. *Question-and-Answer Period:* Allow ample time for questions and answers after the presentation. To encourage spirited audience

participation, plant some provocative questions in advance with the right members. Antagonistic questions and any altercations or heckling must be quickly discouraged.

12. *Afterward:* Protect the speaker from inundation by the audience after the meeting. A flood of people from all parts of the room can be disturbing to someone who has made a long presentation. See that the speaker has an opportunity to rest or leave the room graciously. Thank the speaker. Present the check (obtained from the treasurer before the meeting) at this time. A letter of thanks should follow immediately, together with any additional publicity clippings that the speaker has not already received.

13. *Other Types of Programming:* Much of what has already been said applies to other types of programs as well. Added detail can be found in "Duties of the Convention Committees," Chapter XVII, for programs such as workshops, exhibits and conferences. For contests and other ideas, see "Special Events," Chapter XVIII.

THE RECORDING SECRETARY

As the title implies, it is the job of the recording secretary to keep a record of the group's activities. The secretary takes notes—the minutes—at all executive board meetings and regular meetings of the organization, as well as any other meetings designated by the president. It is important that the minutes be accurate and unbiased. A copy of the minutes is sent to the president as soon as possible after the meeting.

Minutes Book:

1. The secretary should write in and read from a permanently bound book. If the organization wishes the minutes typed, the pages must be numbered as used and the book bound at the end of the administration.

2. The title of the meeting, the organization's name, date, time, and place, and the name and title of the presiding officer should head

the minutes. If there is a parliamentarian, that person's name should also appear in the heading.

3. A short title of each paragraph's subject should appear in the left hand margin. The margin at the right should have sufficient space for corrections and/or additions. (See sample minutes, below.)

4. List in the front of the minutes book:
   a. The bank and the address where the organization's documents are kept.
   b. The number of the key to the safe-deposit box.
   c. The names of the officers who have keys.
   d. If the papers are kept elsewhere, the name of the person who has them.
   e. Charter. All information regarding the original charter or incorporation papers—number, issue date, where it is kept, etc.—also should be recorded in the front of the minutes book. This should be carried over to the new minutes book for reference.

SAMPLE OF MINUTES PAGE

DATE	TITLE OF MEETING	ORGANIZATION NAME
	PLACE	MEETING TIME

Presiding officer   *Parliamentarian*

Call to order	The meeting of the .... was called to order at 2 P.M. by President John Doe.	
Pledge of Allegiance	The pledge of Allegiance was led by Jane Brown at the request of the president.	(This is the column for additions and/or corrections.)
Invocation	Sarah Lee gave the invocation.	
Roll call	(Attendance book or roll sheet should be signed.) Names of members and guests are now entered in the minutes.	

Introduction of guests	Mary Smith introduced Martha Long, a guest at the meeting.
Announcements	President Doe announced that the time for the April meeting had been changed to 3 P.M.
Minutes	The minutes of the previous meeting were approved as read.
Reports	The president called on the vice-president for a report. Mr. White reported that the speaker for the May program would be Tom Long.
Financial statement	Marion Lewis reported a balance of $1,077 in the checking account and $2,824.84 in the savings account.
New members	Membership Chairperson Lois Page reported three new members. They are Jim Witten, Kenneth Lang, and Hester Thorpe.
Rose show	Special Education Chairperson Kitty Wallace gave a report on how the education booth would be set up at the rose show. There will be three members in attendance at all times to help visitors.
Unfinished business	There was none.

Correspondence	Corresponding Secretary Jenny Lowe read a letter from Richard Crewe, asking for a donation to the park planting fund.
New business	Dana Martin moved that we donate $15 to the park planting fund. The motion was seconded and passed.
Adjournment	The meeting was adjourned at 3:15 P.M.

SIGNED_____

Recording secretary

Approval of the Minutes: The minutes are read at the next meeting. After any additions and/or corrections have been made, the word "approved" and the date is written at the end and initialed by the president.

Motions: All motions must be written out and signed by the maker. The secretary records the name of the maker, the exact motion, and the action taken. The written motion is filed in a box under the date of the meeting in which the motion was made.

Attendance: Circulate a roll sheet to record the names of officers, chairpersons, members, and guests present.

Contracts: All contracts must have the signatures of both the president and the recording secretary. A photocopy of each contract should be kept in the recording secretary's current file. Dates of contract renewals should be kept on the secretary's calendar. The secretary advises the treasurer when these must be renewed and paid.

Ready Reference File: The secretary should have the bylaws, rules of order, standing rules, and current motions available at all meetings.

THE CORRESPONDING SECRETARY

The corresponding secretary is responsible for all correspondence of the organization and reads correspondence at meetings, as requested by the president.

Files: All correspondence and carbons of answers should be kept in readily available alphabetical order for reference as needed.

Notice of Meetings: The corresponding secretary should send a notice and agenda of board meetings to all board members in ample time for them to return advice as to whether or not they will attend. Unless notice of regular meetings appears in the newsletter or is given by the telephone committee, a card with the date, time, place, and program of each regular meeting should be sent members.

Agendas: Before each meeting and other functions where it may be necessary, a typed copy of the agenda (see p. 24) should be at the place of each member of the board. At those functions where honored guests, speakers, or members of the executive board are seated, it is a nice courtesy to have an agenda at each place that includes the names and titles of those at the head table, in the order in which they are seated. Some background on the speaker or honored guests will make conversation easier.

Sunshine: Sometimes it falls to the secretary to send out get-well cards, birthday cards, and condolence letters.

THE TREASURER

The treasurer is custodian of all funds of the organization. Bonding the treasurer protects both the treasurer and the organization when large sums of money are involved. Most small organizations do not have this requirement.

Payment of Recurring Bills: Bills for taxes, utilities, rents, service contracts and renewals, salaries, postal permits, and insurance may be handled by the treasurer routinely after the budget items have been approved by the executive board and/or general membership. Salary raises, increased charges on renewals, rents, etc., must be presented to the executive board for approval before being paid.

Checks:
1. Signatures of both the president and the treasurer should be required on each check. Their signatures must be on file at the bank chosen by the organization for checking and saving needs.
2. If desired, the signatures of the vice-president and the assistant treasurer, or recording secretary can be filed at the bank. This is helpful in an emergency, but the additional signatures may not be used without the consent of the executive board.
3. Rubber stamp signatures are *never acceptable* on checks.

Taxes: Applicable local, state, and federal taxes must be paid promptly to avoid costly penalties. (To determine what taxes your organization must pay, see "Taxes," Chapter X.)

Financial Statements: These must be provided for the president, assistant treasurer (if there is one), and the recording secretary not later than one week prior to the executive board meeting. The president can plan the agenda to take into consideration possible expenditures that might depend on the financial condition of the organization. The budget chairperson may request a financial statement to aid in preparing the budget. Special reports may be requested by the executive board at any time.

The following financial statement will work for most organizations. It is important that all receipts and disbursements be itemized. The executive board should not allow the treasurer to make a report that only gives the balance in the treasury.

SAMPLE OF MONTHLY FINANCIAL STATEMENT

NAME OF ORGANIZATION   **NAME OF TREASURER**

ADDRESS OF ORGANIZATION   **ADDRESS AND PHONE NUMBER**

Financial statement of September 1980 ....
Checking account # .... in .... Bank
Branch ....
Address ....

Receipts

Dues	$1,250	for 100 members
Sales	30	plant table
	18	book table
Ads	5	in newsletter
Raffle	25	for plants

Total receipts $1,328

Disbursements

Rent	35	for meeting
Newsletter	22	includes mailing
Refreshments	10	
Plants	20	for raffle
Books	9	for book table
Directory	130	includes some mailing
Speaker	25	

Total disbursements .... $ 251
Balance in checking account $1,077 $1,077.00
Savings Account # ..... Balance $2,789.00
                Interest added Aug. 30   35.84
                                                  $2,824.84
                                    Total $3,901.84

Annual Reports: Annual reports of the contributors, contributions, income, and expenditures of the organization should be available to members.

Bookkeeping Procedures:

1. A system should be agreed upon with the auditor, and set up after the approval of the executive board.

2. Any changes in the system to facilitate the processes of book-keeping must have the approval of the auditor, the budget chairperson, and the executive board.

3. Records of all deposits, receipts, and disbursements must be maintained accurately and up-to-date.

4. Check stubs must be balanced with each check written and deposit made.

Dues:

1. The treasurer keeps a record of each payment of dues.

2. Notice of dues payment date must be given to members in ample time (usually several months ahead), either by mail or in the newsletter, or both.

3. The treasurer must advise a member in writing that dues are late before the member can be dropped for nonpayment of dues.

Master Card File: This is usually the responsibility of the treasurer and is a practical method of listing all changes, additions, and records of dues payments. A list in a book, with the many changes that must be made, can become confusing and leave untidy records. Cards, on the other hand, can be changed and new ones added without disturbing the rest of the file.

1. Prepare a separate card for each member. (See sample below.)

2. Add full address, zip code, and telephone number.

3. Offices held and the years of administration should be included.

4. Space should be provided to record payment of dues. This should be set up by years with a place to enter the date and amount.

5. The back of the card provides a space to add helpful information, such as other affiliations, occupation, hobbies, or connec-

tions with the media for publicity purposes, if the organization does not use a Skills Inventory Card.

6. File the cards alphabetically by last names.

SAMPLE MASTER CARD

NAME	OFFICES HELD	YEAR	AMOUNT	ARREARS
Doe, John	Treasurer 1979–80	1979	$12	
1 Place Street		1980	$15	
Anytown, State 00000				
Tel: 777–7777				

Resignations and Members Dropped: They should be reported to the corresponding secretary, the newsletter editor, and the telephone chairperson. File resigned and dropped members' cards in a separate file. Some of them may reapply for membership.

Deaths: These must be reported to the president, the editor, corresponding secretary, and telephone chairperson. File cards in archives.

Membership Directory: It is made up from the *paid-up* list that the treasurer provides for the chairperson. It includes the corrected addresses, marriage status (where that applies), and any titles.

Audit: All financial records should be available to the auditor five days prior to audit.

Chapter VI

Duties of Committee Chairpersons

Committees are groups of members of an organization charged with specific duties or responsibilities. Most of the work of an organization is done by committee, except for those duties delegated to the officers.

Many nonprofit corporations, societies, and clubs arbitrarily classify committees as "standing" and "special" and deny special committee chairpersons a vote or voice on the executive board. For example: in one nationwide group, the workshop chairperson is classed as the head of a special committee and is deprived of voice or vote of the executive board. This chairperson has a committee of six people, living in all parts of the country. With their assistance, this committee head plans workshops for conventions and encourages workshop activity in over 200 branches.

Other groups put the chairpersons of fund-raisers, special events, and conventions into the "special committee" category, even though these events take place year after year, and these chairpersons are among the hardest workers in the organization.

We recommend that organizations take a close look at committees they designate as "special." If the committee continues to function for one administration after another, the chairperson should be a member of the executive board. Committees that are appointed to bring back a report or to make a study or investigation and are then disbanded after a few months should be considered "special committees."

If the bylaws specify standing committees by name, we recommend that they be changed. The bylaws should empower the president, with approval of the elected officers, to appoint committee heads necessary to carry out the organization's work. The specific committees should be listed in the rules of order. (See "Bylaws and How to Write Them," Chapter III.)

Committees Usually Needed: In most organizations, committee chairpersons are appointed for budget, program, membership, membership directory, newsletter, telephone, hospitality, public relations, nominating, fund-raising, and special events. The program and public relations chairpersons and newsletter editor can function alone. In a small organization (20 members or less), only one person is needed to telephone. In a larger group, committee members share the calling.

Optional Committees: Additional committees are appointed depending upon the organization's purposes and activities. A social service or community-support group may need a volunteer coordinator. Political action, ecology, and conservation organizations frequently appoint a legislative committee to monitor state and local government meetings. An organization with a headquarters or clubhouse may find a committee to supervise the building necessary. A swim and tennis club may want to appoint committees responsible for the swim team, pool maintenance, and tennis competition. If books are owned, a librarian is needed. In some organizations, the parliamentarian, auditor, historian, and librarian are elected; in others, they are appointed by the president. We have included their duties in this chapter because we feel that these positions, if necessary to the organization, are best filled by appointment. The nominating committee may have problems filling the usual slate and does not need the added burden of finding members for these positions.

Appointments: The president appoints the committee heads with the approval of the other elected officers. The appointments are made as soon as possible after election. An elected officer can head a committee. The vice-president is often asked to take charge of program planning, and the treasurer may be appointed head of the budget committee.

Many organizations elect the nominating committee, either during regular elections or at a meeting three or four months prior to elections. This is done so that the president, through appointment of friends, will not control nominations to office. (See "Bylaws and How to Write Them, Chapter III.)

General Duties of Committee Heads: Except for special committees appointed for short periods of time, the committee heads are members of the executive board. They are expected to attend board meetings and report on their activities. They should hold planning sessions with their committee members, seek their advice, and allocate responsibilities to them. At the end of the administration, all records and files are turned over to the incoming chairpersons.

Committee Members: The members of the various committees may be appointed by the president or by the committee chairperson, whichever the group desires.

If the president makes the appointments, the names are submitted to the chairperson for approval before asking the proposed members to serve. The rejection of a name should be accepted without comment. Mary Smith may have good reason for not wanting Tom Long or Jane Jones on her committee, but she may not want to discuss it. If the chairperson makes the appointments, the president's approval is obtained first.

Qualifications: The abilities, interests, talents, and personalities of members should be considered by the person making the appointments. Members with limited time may willingly serve on the budget or directory committee where their duties will be completed early in the administration. An older or house-bound member can be made to feel valuable by being asked to take charge of telephoning (for a small group) or serving on the committee, if the group is a large one.

While the ability to write is an asset to the newsletter editor and the public relations chairperson, many organizations make the mistake of always asking writers to take these jobs. Most artists do not like to make table favors, and many writers shudder at doing publicity even when they are approached with, "But you can do it so easily, and you'd be so good at it." Frequently, artists and writers are reluctant to join groups other than professional ones because of this. The person who wants to write, but has not yet started, can make the perfect public relations chairperson. The professional writer can be asked to help as an adviser.

If possible, the membership chairperson should be a longtime resident who is active in the community. A warm, gregarious person who loves to meet people makes a good hospitality chairperson. The inclusion of a shy, retiring member on this committee may help that person to develop qualities of leadership. It's easier to be friendly with a "Hospitality Committee" badge pinned on the shoulder.

A member should be invited to head a committee. A refusal should be graciously accepted; coercion should never be used.

Considerations for Acceptance:

1. A job description should be supplied the member invited to head a committee.

2. Members should thoroughly understand their duties and consider the time and effort required before acceptance.

3. The opportunity for personal growth, service to the community, and advancement in the organization are often rewards of heading committees.

4. It is the member's responsibility to carry out the duties dependably, efficiently, and punctually. If a change in health, family, or job situation prevents this, a prompt resignation should be offered or assistance requested.

Duties of the Budget Chairperson: (See "Your Budget," Chapter VIII.)

Duties of the Program Chairperson: (See "Duties of Other Officers," Chapter V.)

THE MEMBERSHIP CHAIRPERSON

This position is among the most important in an organization. Unless new people are encouraged to join, the membership will inevitably decline, because people move, die, or become inactive for reasons of health, family, or business problems, or simply lose interest. The organization needs to maintain a positive, friendly approach toward new people. The group that says "We don't want to get too large" can find itself so small after a few years that it is difficult to get a quorum out to a meeting.

How to Start: Immediately after accepting the appointment, the chairperson sets up a meeting with the committee members, the president, and the public relations chairperson to discuss goals and outline a campaign.

Membership Campaign: The membership campaign can consist of meetings that are open to the public, luncheons, dinners, special program or achievement meetings to which prospective members are invited, and personal contact, depending upon the organization's standards for membership. A brochure explaining the organization's goals and activities can be prepared. (See "Public Relations," Chapter XIV.) Growth of an organization is not solely the membership committee's responsibility. A concerted effort by every member to interest new people will aid the campaign.

Admission Policy: The organization's policy and procedures for admission to membership should be thoroughly understood by all members. It is extremely embarrassing to encourage a person to attend a meeting only to find out later that the person is ineligible to become a member.

Membership Qualifications: The membership chairperson must be thoroughly familiar with the qualifications for membership. If special requirements must be met, as in many professional organizations, the applicant's credentials must be screened. However, membership in nonprofit incorporations cannot be denied because of race or sex. Some groups require that a prospective member be introduced at two or three meetings. Others require sponsorship by an active member. These requirements should be detailed in the bylaws.

Open Membership: If membership is open to anyone interested, dues must be accepted from anyone desiring to join.

Introduction of Prospective Members: The membership chairperson introduces prospective members at an appropriate time during the meeting. Usually some information is given to the membership about the prospect.

Invitation to Join: The chairperson must extend an invitation to join to prospective members. Many times an interested, but shy person attends an organization's meetings two or three times and then is not seen again because, "No one asked me to join. I decided they did not want me."

Membership Applications: The applications can be extremely detailed, as in the case of professional or scientific organizations requiring proof of a specified level of achievement or may simply ask for the applicant's name, address, and phone number.

It is the membership chairperson's responsibility to see that the application is filled out accurately and completely. If endorsers or sponsors are required, the chairperson should check with the treasurer to see that the persons signing as such are members in good standing with dues paid to date.

Voting: In organizations in which applicants for membership must be approved by vote, usually the bylaws only call for approval of the executive board or approval by the board before vote by the general membership. Personal prejudice should not influence the vote. Applicants should be judged solely on the basis of whether or not they meet the standards for membership.

How to Handle the Ineligible Applicant: Membership qualifications can include such things as residence in a certain geographic area or the attainment of a specified professional level. Ineligible applicants can be told by the membership chairperson that they do not meet the requirements. Some organizations, such as writers, artists, and crafts groups have a category of provisional membership. Applicants who show promise are admitted to that category for a limited time. The active members advise and help the provisionals, usually through workshops and critique sessions, to meet the qualifications for full membership.

How to Handle the Undesirable Applicant: Fortunately, this problem does not often arise, but it can be one of the touchiest situations that organizations that accept applicants to membership by vote can face. This type of organization usually requires that the applicant be introduced to the general membership twice before an application is submitted, and that two active members sign the application as sponsors.

If a member has personal knowledge that the prospective member has been guilty of professional dishonesty, it is that member's duty to inform the membership chairperson of that fact. In that case the prospective member is not invited to join and is not given a membership application.

If an undesirable applicant has submitted an application for membership, it is the duty of members who have first-hand knowledge of professional or criminal actions sufficient to disqualify the applicant, to lay these facts before the executive board. We caution members to be certain of their facts. It can be unpleasant to be sued for slander.

It is vital that the situation be kept confidential. If denied election to membership, the applicant should be informed by letter that the executive board regrets that the application does not meet the organization's standards. If pressed by a pushy applicant for specific reasons, the board should simply reiterate its statement and refuse to discuss the matter further.

We emphasize that personalities, gossip, or hearsay should not enter into discussion of an applicant's eligibility. Mutual antipathy can change to mutual admiration when two people work together on a worthwhile project. However, once or twice during an organization's existence it will be faced with a situation where an applicant must be denied membership. The executive board should understand this and be prepared to handle the situation. It is far easier to deny an applicant membership than to go through discipline procedures resulting in expulsion of a member from the group.

Introduction of New Members: New members should be introduced to the organization and formally presented with their membership cards at the next meeting.

Distribution of Names: Names, addresses, and telephone numbers of new members are distributed to the president, treasurer, corresponding secretary, telephone chairperson, and newsletter editor. They are published in the next newsletter.

Skills Inventory Card: The president and committee heads are helped if the new member fills out a Skills Inventory Card indicating areas of interest, occupation, and past experience. Completion of this card can be optional.

SKILLS INVENTORY CARD

Name: _____ Address: _____ Tel: _____

Occupation: _____ Hobbies: _____

Past Experience: _____   _____

_____   _____

Affiliations: _____ Special Interests: _____

_____   _____

Committee Preference: _____

Membership File: A file is kept of interested prospects and persons who have decided against joining the organization. This file is turned over to the next chairperson.

DUTIES OF THE MEMBERSHIP DIRECTORY CHAIRPERSON

The directory is compiled immediately after election and payment of dues. The names of paid-up members are obtained from the treasurer. If the group is not too large, one person should be able to prepare the directory.

Contents: The directory includes the name of the organization, name, address, and telephone number of each member in alphabetical order. Some groups include the spouse's name in parenthesis if the member is married. If the member's profession entitles him/her to be addressed by title, this is used. Honorary degrees are not considered titles. Example:

Jones, Dr. Mary Lou (Robert), 110 West Main St. Bigtown, NY 99999 426-4795
Keyes, John (Helen), 100 Branch Dr. Westcity, OR 04040 291-2691

Officers and heads of committees are listed. The programs scheduled for the administration and the date, place, and times of regular meetings are included if possible.

Format: The directory can be photocopied, mimeographed, or printed. For small organizations the material can be laid out on 8½ × 11 paper so that the pages can be folded in half and stapled together by the members. This helps to keep down costs. It is necessary to plan the layout carefully so that the directory can be put together in alphabetical order.

Organizations with thousands of members may want to have the

directory printed. Since the expense of binding can be great and the pages are apt to fall out if the binding is glued, we recommend that the directory be printed on 6 × 8 three-hole paper so that it can be placed in a 7 × 9 three-ring binder purchased by the member. In either case, it is important that space be allowed for the addition of new members' names and addresses, so that the directory will not be out-dated too soon.

Distribution: The directory is distributed to every member each year or two, depending upon the length of the administration. The directory should not be sold to mail-order firms or loaned to other organizations without prior approval of the executive board.

DUTIES OF THE TELEPHONE CHAIRPERSON

It is the telephone chairperson's responsibility to notify members of the date, place, and time of regular or special meetings, as well as relay other information to members as requested by the president. This might include such things as asking for donations to a bake sale or notifying members of a home-owners' association about a proposed zoning change.

Procedure: Prepare the message ahead of time, so it is clear and brief. Say what you have to say, and get off the telephone.

Time: The best times to find members at home are before 9 A.M. and during the dinner hour. They won't object to the interruption *if* you are brief. If you consistently find a person hard to reach, ask what is the best time to call or send a postcard.

Committee: If working with a committee, relay the message to the members and give them the deadline for completing the calls. Divide the telephoning by alphabet or by telephone zones to avoid toll charges.

Warning: Don't depend upon children to relay messages.

DUTIES OF THE HOSPITALITY CHAIRPERSON

This committee is in charge of the guest book, name tags, refreshments, and greeting guests at the door. The duties should be rotated with each meeting, so that no member is constantly stuck in the kitchen.

Greeting: Guests and new members are welcomed at the door. If possible, they are immediately introduced to several members.

Guest Book: Guests are requested to sign the guest book. Their names and addresses are turned over to the membership chairperson after each meeting.

Name Tags: Name tags are distributed. An attendance record can be obtained from the unclaimed name tags instead of passing an attendance sheet.

Refreshments: A committee member prepares coffee, tea, and refreshments (if served) and sets up a table with cups, spoons, sugar, cream, and napkins. During the refreshment period, all members of the committee should be alert, so that no shy guest or new member is left standing alone in a corner.

DUTIES OF THE NOMINATING COMMITTEE

(For size, selection, and people to nominate, as well as the method of determining a committee chairperson, see "Bylaws and How to Write Them," Chapter III.)

General Considerations:
1. Members of the committee should thoroughly familiarize themselves with the duties of the officers.
2. All discussion of the committee is kept confidential.

3. The names of those selected for nomination are not made public before the committee makes its report at the designated time and place.

4. Serving on the committee does not make a member ineligible for nomination to office.

Choosing the President: If the vice-president has been doing a good job, this person should be considered first. In some groups elevation of the vice-president to the presidency is automatic. Qualities to look for are leadership, ability to get along with people and to delegate authority, warmth, friendliness, reliability, experience, interest in the organization, and self-confidence.

Vice-President: The committee must remember that this person may be the next president and will have to serve if the president is ill or absent. Planning programs can be this officer's responsibility.

Recording Secretary: Must be able to attend every meeting. Should have good hearing and ability to take unbiased minutes.

Corresponding Secretary: Should have ability to write clear letters. In an organization that is grant or tax-supported, all or in part, this person may have the responsibility of making reports to funding agencies or writing grant proposals.

Treasurer: This officer should have the ability to handle figures and be good at record-keeping.

Procedure: Once the committee has decided upon a slate of officers, the chairperson calls the nominees, starting with the president, to get acceptance. Never call anyone for another office until a president has accepted.

What to Do If the Committee Is Divided and Cannot Agree: Two slates can be submitted to the membership. However, the nominees should be informed that this will be done. A minority report can be submitted by members of the committee. Committee members can make nominations from the floor when nominations are open during the meeting.

The Report: The president asks for the report of the nominating committee at a meeting prescribed in the bylaws. The chairperson reads the report without comment.

Presenting Qualifications: Qualifications of nominees may be presented to the members in the newsletter or house organ. The chairperson informs the candidates of the deadline and required information.

THE PARLIAMENTARIAN

The duties of the parliamentarian are few, but important to the organization. The parliamentarian serves as adviser to the president in all matters pertaining to the rules of conduct contained in the articles of incorporation or organization, constitution, bylaws, rules of order and standing rules. It is very important that the parliamentarian be well acquainted with these rules.

DUTIES OF THE AUDITOR

The auditor of a small organization may be appointed by the president. If possible, the member should have some bookkeeping knowledge. Where many funds (endowments, scholarships, building, etc.) are involved, a professional auditor should be employed. In either case, the auditor should consult with the current treasurer to establish a system of bookkeeping that will serve the organization properly.

Time: Audit of the books and accounts of the treasurer may be made semiannually, or annually, and at such times as the president directs. The books must be made available to the auditor at least five days prior to the date of audit.

Procedure: The auditor must be satisfied that:

1. There is adequate documentation (receipts, bills, vouchers, etc.) to back up all expenditures and income.

2. There is proper ledger posting of income and expenditures.

3. Bank reconciliations are timely.

4. Unrecorded liabilities do not exist.

5. Withholding taxes, that need to be paid are being deducted.

6. One or more bank statements can be reconciled with checkbook stubs, deposit slips, etc.

The Report: It should be concise and should indicate the extent of the auditor's sampling. It should also include the auditor's opinion of the financial records, and when necessary, recommendations should be made for improved practices. The report is submitted at the next executive board meeting.

DUTIES OF THE HISTORIAN

The historian keeps a record of the achievements, awards, honors, and special events related to the members and the organization.

Scrapbook: News clippings, photographs, and copies of programs, flyers, and brochures are generally included in a scrapbook. This can be helpful when prospective members attend a meeting, because it gives them an idea of the organization's activities.

History: The historian should be familiar with the history of the organization. When called upon, the historian should be able to give a factual narrative, pointing out past events of interest to the members. The headquarters of the organization may have some special features or historical background, which may be a part of the narrative.

Achievements: The historian frequently serves as the achievements chairperson. An achievements sheet is sent around at meetings.

Members list current achievements and sign their names. This list is sent to the editor of the newsletter in ample time for publication.

DUTIES OF THE SCHOLARSHIP CHAIRPERSON

If the organization has a scholarship program, the chairperson is in charge of the selection of recipients of the awards.

Committee: The rules for awarding scholarships are established by a committee which also judges the applicants. The committee is made up of the following people:

1. Two faculty members from a degree-granting institution or institutions. This is an Internal Revenue Service ruling, to which all tax-exempt organizations must adhere.
2. The president of the organization.
3. The treasurer.
4. The public relations chairperson.
5. A legal adviser familiar with scholarship funds.
6. The recording secretary who also takes the minutes.

Applications: The rules should clearly define eligibility requirements for the applicant. All information required by the committee should be listed on the application. This data includes:

1. Official transcripts from the school the applicant now attends and those previously attended.
2. A letter of recommendation from a professor at the school the applicant now attends.
3. Additional letters of recommendation.
4. Full-time enrollment in either a diploma or degree program at an accredited university, college, or community college.
5. Other standards set by the committee such as ethnic background, residence in the same county as the club is located, or enrollment in a specified course of study—for example, gerontology or oceanology.

Screening: One method of screening and judging is this scale.
1. Academics (special study), 40 points
2. Academics (general excellence), 25 points
3. Leadership, 10 points
4. Financial need, 20 points
5. Recommendations, 5 points

Separate evaluation must be made for students who work part-time, because they cannot spend time in extracurricular activities. In the case of two students being equal in points, the student with financial need should be given preference.

Awards:

1. Winners are notified by the committee. Copies of the notification are sent to the president of the winner's school and to individuals who have sent in letters of recommendation.

2. A glossy photograph of the winner, with a biographical sketch should go to the public relations chairperson who sends a news release to local papers with some mention of the organization's scholarship goals.

3. A letter should be sent to students who were not chosen, thanking them, and encouraging them to try again.

4. A check is sent to the school to be attended by the winner, where it is credited to the student's account.

5. Recognition of the winning student at a meeting of the organization can encourage members to make additional contributions to the scholarship program.

DUTIES OF THE LIBRARIAN

The librarian is custodian of all books belonging to the organization's library. It is this chairperson's responsibility to catalogue the collection properly and keep a record of borrowed books.

Library Policy: With the approval of the executive board, the librarian develops a policy for:
1. Length of time books may be kept by the borrower.

2. The number a member can take out at one time.

3. The fine per day or per week for overdue books.

4. The charge for damaged or lost books.

5. The purpose for which fines or charges shall be used.

6. Selection of new books to be purchased for the library.

7. Standards for donations permitting the organization to give away unsuitable books.

8. Standards for discarding out-dated books.

Catalogue Cards: (two or three for each book) must have the following:

1. Name of author.

2. Title of book. (Capitalize only the first letter.)

3. Publisher's name.

4. Year of copyright.

5. Number of pages.

6. Note whether the book contains diagrams, maps, pictures.

7. Indicate whether the book is paperback.

8. Date acquired.

9. Price.

SAMPLE CATALOGUE CARD

SMITH, JANE
  How to grow roses.   Anchor Press,   1980

  225 p. ills.   (paper)

  date acquired
  price

Recommended Filing System:

1. With two cards, file one alphabetically by author (last name first) and file the second alphabetically by title.

2. With three cards, file the third by category of the book (Art, Flowers, Travel) or file as "Art—painting technique" or "Flowers—drying." The third card is necessary only if the library is large.

Ownership of the book should be stamped on the title page and on one other page designated for use on all books. It may be desirable to stamp the book also on the closed edges of the pages.

Maintenance: If there is a permanent home for the library, books should be divided into subject categories and shelved in alphabetical order by authors' names. They can be numbered and shelved according to the Dewey Decimal or any other recognized system, but this is difficult for the librarian who does not have professional training. If the organization has a large library, it may want to hire a professional librarian to catalogue the books and set up a system for the library chairperson to follow.

Where there is no permanent home for the library, storage space will have to be found by the librarian. It may be necessary to divide the books among the homes of the committee members. In this case, an identifying label such as a gold circle should be placed on the spine of each book so it can be easily kept separate from the member's own books. The librarian will need to keep a list of books stored by each committee member.

Making the Books Available to Members:

1. Regular hours and days should be established for a permanent library.

2. If a library housed by members is small, it can be brought to meetings.

3. If a library housed by members contains too many books for easy transportation, the catalogue cards are brought to meetings. Members select books to be brought to the next meeting and returned when due.

Check Out Record Cards:

1. A card is made up for each book headed by the author's name (last name first). The title of the book, date of publication, and price are listed also.

2. Space is needed for the name of the person borrowing the book, the date borrowed, the date returned, and the condition.

3. The card is clipped to the book or placed in a pocket pasted inside the front cover.

4. When the book is borrowed, the card is filled out and placed in the circulation file.

Circulation File: This should be reviewed on a regular basis. When a book becomes past due, the borrower is notified by telephone.

Sharing of Books Owned by Members:

1. A form is sent to members on which they list, by category, books they are willing to lend.

2. The librarian makes this list available at meetings.

3. Members wishing to borrow these books make their own arrangements with the owners.

Chapter VII

The Executive Board

The structure and responsibilities of the executive board should be written into the bylaws. Example: The executive board shall consist of the elected officers and the committee chairpersons. The management and control of the business, funds, and property of the association shall be vested in the executive board.

Meetings: The number of meetings required and the months in which they are to be held may be written into either the bylaws or the standing rules.

Policy and Objectives of the Organization: The executive board has the responsibility of deciding what actions an organization will take to carry out its objectives. This decision is made based on the reports and investigation of officers, chairpersons, or committees. If a group composed of professional writers has as one of its purposes the promotion of creative writing, it might decide that one way of doing this would be to hold a contest for high school seniors. Before the executive board votes to take this action, it should hear a report from the appropriate chairperson regarding the feasibility of the event. Does the organization have the money to finance the contest and make awards? Does it have enough members to do the work? How many schools will have to be contacted? Will private schools be included? Will the English teachers cooperate and urge their students to enter? Who will write the rules? How will the rules be distributed? Who will do the judging? What will be the standards for the judges? How many contests are held each year for high school students? Is the proposed event appropriate to the organization's purpose? Will it generate publicity and enable the group to become better known? Is it a service to the community? Once these questions are answered, the executive board can arrive at a decision.

How the Board Functions: In a small organization most of the members will also be members of the executive board. If the membership meets once a month, it may decide to handle its business at the regular meeting. However, a large organization or one with bylaws that call for only a yearly membership meeting will function better if the business is taken care of at regularly scheduled executive board meetings. The bylaws should give this authority to the board.

First Executive Board Meeting of New Administration:

1. This takes place as soon as possible after installation.
2. The bylaws and job descriptions should be reviewed with the executive board, so that all business of the organization can be consummated with dispatch and understanding.
3. The administration's goals, purposes, and activities are discussed.
4. Committee reports and recommendations for special events and/or fund-raisers are evaluated.
5. The program chairperson outlines the year's programs.
6. The budget chairperson presents the budget for the year.
7. At the next general meeting, the board recommendations are presented to the members for ratification, if the bylaws so require.

Review of the Organization's Progress and Evaluation: Along with setting the policy of an organization, the executive board should review its progress. It is not enough to state in the bylaws that the group's purpose is to focus public attention on library services, facilities, and needs. It is the board's responsibility to evaluate the programs designed to carry out this purpose. How does the organization focus public attention on the needs of the library? Is the program practical, and is it attaining the desired results?

The resources of one library were strained each year by a flood of students requesting the same material, because all the teachers in the city made assignments of the same topic at the same time. When 400 students wanted material on state history the same day, the library could not meet the demand. Resourceful students soon started telephoning their homes with a request that a parent go immediately to the library and get the material. Books and periodicals dealing with the assignments were gone from the library even before the school day ended.

The city librarian discussed the problem with both the library's trustees and the Friends of the Library. A teachers' tea was planned and held at the start of the school year, so that teachers could tour the library. During the tea, the librarian gave a talk explaining the facilities and the great difficulties the library had in dealing with mass assignments. He asked that advance notice be given, so that the books needed could be set aside and restricted to use only in the library. He also asked that the assignments be staggered, so that not all students in the city would be searching for the same information at one time.

When the executive board evaluated the program, the members found that it was unsuccessful because few teachers attended the tea. The board then recommended that a postcard form be developed and distributed to the teachers for their use in notifying the library of mass assignments. They appointed a committee to meet with the superintendent of schools to discuss the problem. As a result of that meeting, a program was developed in which members of the organization went to the schools and discussed the limitations of the library at teachers' meetings.

Finances: It is the responsibility of the executive board to see that the organization's funds are handled properly. The budget or financial committee's report to the board should include projections for the future that will allow the organization to plan for a large expenditure such as the renovation of its meeting hall. Members of the board should assure themselves that the bills are being paid and that contracts and insurance are renewed.

Communications with the General Membership: It is important that board members recognize that they serve on the board as representatives of the membership. People who are not kept informed about what is happening in an organization are not likely to continue to pay dues. Therefore it is necessary that regular reports of the organization's financial condition and its programs and activities be made to members. In a small group this is easily handled, because committee chairpersons and officers usually make reports at each business meeting. It is with the large national organization with a centralized headquarters that this communication can break down, especially if only one membership meeting is held each year. Some organizations require that minutes of executive board meetings or a summary of its actions be published and distributed to all members in the house organ or newsletter. If this is not done, a yearly report should be made.

Duties of Individual Executive Board Members:

1. Attend board meetings. The president should be notified if a member cannot attend. The member must send any reports or necessary information to the president, so that it can be presented at the meeting.

2. Prepare for the meeting. Reports should be written in triplicate. All necessary books and information should be brought to the meeting.

3. Executive board members should understand their own duties and responsibilities. They should be familiar with the organizing articles, bylaws, rules of order, and standing rules.

4. It is easier for the executive board to function smoothly if the members are familiar with the duties of the other officers and chairpersons. Since these duties are written into the bylaws or rules of order, they should be known by all members. Unfortunately, many

organizations have board members who have never seen a copy of the bylaws.

5. Individual board members should bear in mind that election to office is an honor. They serve on the board to represent and act in the best interests of the membership. They should not grind axes or allow self-interest or prejudice to influence their decisions.

6. Officers and chairpersons must remember that they are parts of a whole. The newsletter editor may feel that the newsletter is the most important thing the organization does, and that all money and effort should be directed to improving it. The membership committee may believe that their efforts deserve more recognition. Board members should understand that cooperation is necessary for the group to function properly.

7. The history of the organization and its bylaws should not be used as an argument against progressive change. The old "But we've always done it that way" is heard much too often when a change in record-keeping or procedures is suggested. Outmoded office procedures should be modernized. The bylaws should be reviewed periodically and changed if they prevent an organization from operating the way its members desire.

HANDLING SPECIAL PROBLEMS

The Nonfunctioning Officer or Chairperson: If officers or chairpersons can not carry out their assigned responsibilities, they can be relieved of office by a two-thirds vote of the executive board. This problem does not often arise, because people who cannot do the work usually resign their positions. What is more likely to occur is that the duties are not being performed properly because of the election or appointment of an incapable person or that they are being carried out in slipshod fashion, because the person did not want the office or appointment and was talked into accepting it. In a small organization, this can be a serious problem because the members may be close friends.

Organizations can get into serious difficulty if an incapable person is elected president. It is not always easy for the nominating committee to judge a member's qualifications for office, and incompetent people can be nominated and elected. If this happens, the vice-president should offer assistance, and the past presidents should give counsel and guidance. In many organizations the immediate past president is a member of the executive board for this purpose.

A nonfunctioning treasurer can cause grave problems. The organization's bills must be paid. The president should be immediately aware when the treasurer's duties are not being performed properly, because the president must also sign checks. If the treasurer becomes ill or incapacitated for a period of time, an effort must be made to obtain the books and financial records. An interim treasurer can be appointed, or resignation of the treasurer can be requested, so that a new one can be appointed.

If the duties of a committee chairperson are not being handled properly, the president should look for the reason. Perhaps the work involved is too much for one person and an assistant or cochairperson is necessary. If poor health or family problems are making it difficult for a chairperson to function properly, the president can suggest tactfully that a resignation would be in that person's best interests. If the chairperson does not accept this graceful way out of the situation, the president can ask for a resignation or request that the executive board take that action.

A Divided Board: At times an executive board can become divided, with some members pushing hard for a certain action and another faction opposed. Unless an immediate decision is necessary, the president should suggest that the business under discussion be studied further. While the wishes of the majority should prevail, a 51 to 49 percent majority leaves almost half of the members opposed. It is best to delay and try to get the group to reach a compromise or consensus of opinion.

Discipline: If charges of professional dishonesty, working against the interests of the organization and/or injuring the professional standing of another member are brought against a member, the executive board has the unpleasant duty of investigating the charges and taking action, if necessary. Falsification of credentials that make a person eligible for membership can be one charge.

Fortunately such situations do not often occur. However, at times it is necessary to take action or risk the breakup of an entire organization.

Confidentiality: Executive board meetings should be open to any member who wishes to attend, although some large groups limit attendance to branch and state presidents. The board may elect to meet in closed session if it is discussing charges brought against a member. A meeting in which a paid employee of the organization is being evaluated should also be closed to everyone except members of the board. Discussions of contracts and insurance should not be open to the general membership, because of the possibility that one of the members could be an employee of a company under consideration. While the action decided upon in executive session may be announced, the discussion should be kept confidential.

REPORTS

All officers and chairpersons are required to make reports at each board meeting. Reports should be made up in triplicate, one copy for the president, one for the files of the recording secretary, and one for the writer's file. Reports should include the following:

1. Name and title. (Chairperson of . . . . . . Committee.)
2. Date.
3. Reference title. (What the report is about.)
4. Goals of the committee.
5. An outline of the activities of the committee since the last report, in as few words as possible.
6. A list of the results of such activities.
7. Plans for future action.
8. A separate financial statement, with copies for the treasurer and budget chairperson, if money is an essential part of the report.
9. Any changes in the makeup of the committee.

Officers who have reports to make should follow the same format. Generally, the vice-president reports on program plans, the recording secretary on the date the minutes were mailed, and the corresponding secretary on "sunshine" activity. The treasurer's report is a financial statement. (See "Duties of Other Officers," Chapter V.)

It is important that reports be brief and to the point. Officers and chairpersons who get to their feet and spend 10 minutes relating the great difficulty they had in carrying out their duties, waste the board's time.

Chapter VIII

Your Budget: A Plan for the Present and a Guide for the Future

With the formation of an organization comes the immediate need for a financial plan. A budget to plan and control expenditures is as necessary for the local organization of 20 gardeners as it is for a nationwide one with 10,000 motorcyclists as members. Without a plan, it is far too easy for a group to spend money impulsively, without considering whether the expenditure is appropriate to its purposes. A budget is a guide to the future, a tool that puts your organization on a sound financial basis, whether your objectives are an annual awards dinner or the donation of playground equipment.

Officers and chairpersons can operate more efficiently when they know how much money they are allowed. Without a budget, committee members may be reluctant to submit small bills for stationery, postage, and telephone calls, bearing the expense themselves. This establishes a bad precedent, since some well-qualified members may refuse to head committees or accept nomination for office because they fear it will be a financial burden. The affluent member who wants to make a contribution above dues can do it by donating the money directly.

How to Plan Your Finances: Initial fees and yearly dues will be determined by the new organization's objectives. For example, if a group of 150 condominium owners decides to organize, are the reasons for organization lack of repairs and maintenance, or the failure of the builder to replace faulty equipment or provide promised recreational facilities? Will the group have to hire interim gardening help? Are the services of a lawyer necessary? Is there free meeting space available, or will it have to be rented? Is a newsletter essential to keep members interested in and aware of the organization's problems and progress? Should the group incorporate? Will there be different classes of membership?

The organizers should come prepared to discuss these kinds of questions and be able to give estimates of costs, or an executive committee should be appointed immediately to investigate costs and procedures. If fast action is required, a second meeting can be scheduled within a few days so that the group can decide whether the prospective course of action is feasible.

Initiation Fees: Initial fees may have to be set higher than yearly dues, to provide a sound financial basis. Sometimes the persons most interested in getting the group off the ground will bear some of the organizing expense. It is not fair to ask persons who earn their living at a profession to donate these services to help form an organization. However, they may offer their services at a reduced rate.

Dues: If at all possible, dues should be set high enough to cover ordinary running expenses. The organization should not collect dues in excess of expenses from its members; its purpose should not be to make a profit from them.

Dues should not be set so high that they keep desirable people from joining. In an effort to keep dues low, small organizations may engage in internal fund-raising, which provides a service to members and, at the same time, puts a small profit in the treasury. Doll clubs may buy ribbons, lace, clay, etc. at wholesale and offer them to members at a small profit. Writers' groups can purchase paper, typewriter ribbons, and envelopes in quantity and sell them to members at a discount. Garden clubs may sell plants and use the profit for horticultural books. Services such as these also encourage membership.

The Budget Chairperson: The president should appoint the chairperson as soon as possible after election. This member needs to be familiar with the organization's activities, purposes, and objectives, and have some financial expertise.

The Budget Committee Meeting:

1. The president, treasurer (if not a member of the committee), and committee members should be notified by the chairperson of the date, time, and place of the budget committee meeting.

2. All officers and committee chairpersons are asked to submit a list of proposed expenditures before the meeting.

SAMPLES OF PROPOSED EXPENDITURES

Telephone chairperson:	None. Calls are local.
Newsletter editor:	Postage $36.00
	Paper 1.50
	Photocopy 14.40
	TOTAL $51.90

3. The chairperson should check the treasurer's records for the past year for all other regular expenses of the group. Examples are rent for a meeting room, travel and luncheon or dinner expenses for the president, office supplies, postal permit, refreshments, or annual awards. It will be necessary to estimate increased costs to cover inflation. If the group is brand new, the budget committee can get some idea of probable expenses by looking at the budgets of comparable organizations to which they belong or draw upon the experience of the other members.

4. A tentative budget that includes all running expenses of the organization should be prepared before the meeting.

5. An estimate of all regular income is provided by the treasurer.

6. Discussion of proposed expenditures and projected income takes place at the committee meeting.

7. If income does not cover expenses, the officers and heads of committees may have to reduce their budgets. If necessary, a recommendation may be made that dues be raised. However, estimated

expenses should not be arbitrarily revised without giving committee chairpersons a chance to defend their requests.

8. Provision should be made for an emergency or reserve fund.

9. The committee's proposed budget is submitted to the executive board and then to the general membership (if the bylaws so direct) for approval. This procedure saves time at subsequent business meetings because bills for items already approved do not have to be placed on the agenda.

10. Money for special projects, such as scholarships, support of local hospitals, playground equipment, etc., should not be considered in the yearly operating budget. Such projects are supported by fund-raising, either external or internal, not by dues.

11. Copies of the approved budget go to the treasurer, president, and recording secretary.

12. A copy of the budget should be available to anyone who asks for it.

13. It is not necessary that all budgeted monies be spent.

14. The president and the executive board must be sure that the organization is following the budget.

SAMPLE BUDGET FOR A SMALL ORGANIZATION

INCOME: Dues	$300	**EXPENSES:**	
ASSETS: Checking	28	Newsletter	$52
	$328	President's fund	30
		Speakers' fees	100
		Refreshments	18
		Stationery	5
		Postage	10
		Rental for meeting space	90
		Reserve fund	23
INCOME AND ASSETS:	$328	Total expense	$328
Restricted fund for scholarship			$356
Scholarship award recommendation			300
Scholarship reserve fund			$ 56

This budget is easily adaptable. Cooperative buying groups would substitute such things as paper bags for stationery, gasoline or truck rental for transportation of goods bought at wholesale for speakers' fees. Condominium owners' associations could have such budget items as a lawyer's retainer, maintenance, and gardener's charges.

While many organizations have no restricted funds, those with endowments, bequests, or fund-raising projects for special purposes must show the funds separately, not as a part of operating expenses. In the sample, the organization raises about $350 yearly for scholarships. The fund is not restricted to the use of interest. (See "Finances," Chapter XI.)

Naturally, large organizations with many members, or those owning real estate, publishing a house organ, or renting an office will have much more detailed budgets. Budgets of large organizations can be further complicated by special funds such as endowments for future building, scholarship bequests, awards donations, etc. These funds are dealt with in detail in Chapter XI. However, the budget chairperson will have to show projections for the funds in the budget.

A budget committee is appointed to handle planning of running expense. Administration of special funds may be the responsibility of various financial committees. The treasurer, assistant treasurer, and the auditor work closely with these committees.

National organizations with large memberships and smaller groups owning property, such as private swim and tennis clubs, will need office help and the services of a paid auditor to make certain that monies are handled efficiently and properly. They may also need legal assistance with tax problems. However, the budget, which is a planning guide, is prepared by the committee as outlined under duties of the budget chairperson and approved by a majority of the executive board or the general membership as set forth in the by-laws. A financial report should be made available to the members at the end of the fiscal year.

SAMPLE BUDGET FOR LARGE ORGANIZATION

ANTICIPATED INCOME:

Members dues, 6,000 at $15	$90,000
New members, 200 at $15	3,000
Initiation fees, 200 at $5	1,000
	$94,000

INVESTMENTS:

Interest	$3,050	
Dividends	1,250	4,300

HEADQUARTERS BUILDING:

Rentals, social events	$300	
Rentals, rooms	3,500	3,800

PUBLICATIONS:

Magazine sales	$125	125

TOTAL ANTICIPATED INCOME:	$102,225

EXPENSES:

ADMINISTRATIVE:

Audit fee	$1,000
Insurance, workmen's compensation	261
Postage	1,000
President's travel, discretionary fund	4,500
Office supplies and services:	
Policy pamphlet	500
Printed stationery	2,050
Annual meeting minutes	500
Salaries:	
Office secretary	8,000
Payroll taxes	936
Telephone:	2,000

Committee expenditures:

Membership	2,400
Recording secretary	500
Treasurer	300
Awards	800
Scholarship	200
	$24,947

PUBLICATIONS:

Membership directory	
Printing	$7,000
Mailing	1,800
Magazine	
Printing 10 issues per year	19,640
Layout	1,900
Address changes	500
Mailing service and permit	1,700
Editor's allowance	1,800
Copyright fee	120
Postage	2,200
Postage return	175
	$36,835

HEADQUARTERS BUILDING:

Utilities:		
Oil and service contract	$2,025	
Gas	135	
Electric	875	
Water and sewage	125	
Garbage	100	3,260
Insurance:		
Fire and theft	1,845	
Liability	275	2,120
Laundry:	250	250
Supplies and equipment	2,750	2,750
(Includes air conditioner service contract)		

Repairs and maintenance	500	500
(Includes painting two rooms)		
Salaries:		
Cleaning service	1,800	
Janitor/yard work	500	
Payroll tax	300	2,600
Taxes:		
Real estate	2,500	
Personal property	65	2,565
Loan repayment:	11,052	
(Emergency noninterest loan from member		
for new furnace and rewiring.)		11,052
		$25,097

TOTAL ANTICIPATED INCOME:	$102,225
TOTAL ANTICIPATED EXPENSES:	86,879
EXCESS OF INCOME OVER EXPENSES:	$15,326

SPECIAL FUNDS:

Headquarters Restoration: $26,750
*(Restricted fund with yearly interest, to be used
for improvements and repair of headquarters
other than routine repair and maintenance.)*
Scholarship fund: 8,300
*(Restricted fund with yearly interest, used for
scholarships to persons over 35 reentering
college.)*

RECOMMENDATIONS OF COMMITTEE: With a surplus of $15,326, the
committee makes the following recommendations to the executive
board:

1. That $10,000 be transferred to the Headquarters Restoration
Fund, which will increase the fund to $36,750. That $30,000 of
this fund be invested in Money Market Certificates. This will
increase the interest income to over $3,000. This amount with the
$1,471 in interest paid this year should cover the new roof, which

the house committee deems necessary next year. The increased amount should make emergency loans from members unnecessary.

2. That $2,000 be transferred to the Scholarship Fund.

3. The budget committee notes that, with an income of over $15,000 in excess of expense this year, the organization is in sound financial shape. However, the committee warns that inflation and the increasing cost of fuel oil will undoubtedly cut into this surplus in future years. Higher prices for printing and postage will drive up the costs of our publications. While the committee recognizes the importance of keeping the general membership informed of the organization's activities, it urges the executive board to look into less expensive means of communication.

This budget can be adapted easily to the use of organizations owning recreational facilities, by adding the costs of their maintenance. The salaries of an activities director and club manager may be added. Costs of a team are generally met by dues charged those participating and by entry fees for meets.

Either the budget committee, the financial committee, or the executive board can make projections for the future, to keep the organization on a sound financial basis. In this example, the budget committee makes the recommendations.

It is the responsibility of the executive board to leave enough money in the treasury to cover all unpaid bills at the end of its term of office. It is also the responsibility of the board to look far enough into the future so that the entire expense of a large repair to a building does not fall solely upon one administration. The expense should be prorated over several administrations.

Chapter IX

Incorporation

Your neighborhood revitalization association has grown to 90 members during its first year. The members have cleared trash from vacant lots and urged the city to repair potholes in the streets. Now Mrs. Lawrence wants to finance the donation of 50 books to the branch library. Mr. Ellis urges that they replant one block of a nearby park. An enthusiastic member proposes that the group do both and finance the ventures by soliciting donations to hold a giant rummage sale.

"We'll have to rent a store. What if someone gets hurt?" Mr. Worrier asks.

"We'll have to pay taxes on our profits," Mrs. Jackson warns.

"I send all my donations to the Long Society. I need the deductions," Miss Page adds.

Gloom settles over the room. "There must be something we can do," the president says. "We aren't a money-making organization. Other clubs have fund-raisers and ask for donations. How can they do it?"

"They are tax-exempt," Miss Page answers. "They are incorporated as nonprofit organizations."

"That's the answer," the president says. "We need a committee to look into incorporating our association."

Corporation: An association of individuals can incorporate under the authority of state law. A corporation is an artificial legal being created by law that can make contracts, incur debts, and pay taxes. It has a continuous existence irrespective of, and with powers and liabilities distinct from, those of its individual members. Most states have a general corporations code that lists requirements. Some states have several corporation codes. One may be for profit corporations; another for nonprofit or charitable corporations. Organizations that satisfy the requirements and file the necessary papers with the proper state authority can become corporations.

Nonprofit Tax-Exempt Corporation: This is a corporation organized for nonprofit activity, with purposes that qualify it for exemption from payment of federal corporate income taxes. (See "Taxes," Chapter X.)

THE ADVANTAGES OF BECOMING A NONPROFIT CORPORATION

Limited Liability: Lawsuits can be filed only against the assets of the nonprofit corporation, not against the property of those who manage, belong to, or work for it. If a nonprofit corporation cannot pay its bills, it can be sued for the money by its debtors, but its owners cannot be sued. A person can lose the money put into a nonprofit corporation (the cost of membership and dues), but not personal money.

Tax Exemption: A nonprofit corporation can apply for tax-exempt status from the Internal Revenue Service.

Tax Deductions: Contributors to nonprofit corporations with tax-exempt status from the Internal Revenue Service can claim personal federal income tax deductions of up to 50 percent of adjusted gross income.

Obtaining Grants: Most foundations and governmental agencies require that an organization applying for funding be a nonprofit tax-exempt corporation.

Increased Membership: People are more likely to join an organization that is a nonprofit, tax-exempt corporation because of the limited legal liability. They recognize that the organization's articles of incorporation and bylaws meet state requirements and that the group must maintain proper records, keep its minutes up to date, and abide by its bylaws.

Increased Status in the Community: Local governmental and other groups know that they are dealing with an organization set up under the law and abiding by legal regulations. They know that the group's purpose must be stated in the articles of incorporation and must be lawful and tax-exempt.

Nonprofit Organization Postage Permit: The nonprofit corporation can apply for bulk-rate mailing privileges.

THE DISADVANTAGES OF BECOMING A NONPROFIT CORPORATION

Political Activity: An organization with tax-exempt status may not work for or against a candidate for political office. Federal regulations also limit the amounts an organization can spend on lobbying to influence legislation or to influence public opinion. Since the laws and rulings are being changed constantly, your organization needs the advice of a tax attorney if it is engaged in lobbying.

Membership Restrictions: Standards for membership are set in the bylaws. According to law, they may not discriminate by race or sex. Your organization does have a right to require qualifications for membership, which may include a geographical area for a neighborhood improvement society, publication for a writing group, or exhibition in juried shows for an artists' club.

Restriction on Activities: An organization cannot engage in unrelated business activity that does not further its tax-exempt purposes and results in "substantial" profit. For example: the Riverview Improvement Association could ask for donations and hold a flea-market sale and use the profits to buy seeds and plants for the park it wants to renovate. If it decided to establish a bakery and use the profits to send the officers on a trip to Europe, the group's tax-exempt status would be endangered.

Restriction on Members' Benefits: No part of a nonprofit corporation's earnings can be distributed to its members. This does not mean that proper salaries or expenses of directors, officers, or members cannot be paid, but their duties must be to carry out the purposes of the corporation.

Size or Scope of Activity: Your organization may be so small or your activity so limited that there is no need for formal organization or incorporation.

Dissolution: This is provided for by the laws of the state in which you incorporate. An organization should be certain that it is going to stay in existence for many years if it incorporates, because the law requires that in the event the group dissolves its assets must be given to a like nonprofit organization.

HOW TO INCORPORATE

Committee Investigation: It is wise to appoint a committee to investigate incorporation. The commitee will have to consider such things as a proper name, the purposes, and legal assistance. Incorporation is handled by the various states, and the laws differ in each one. The committee should write to the proper state authority, requesting all information, pamphlets, and sample articles of incorporation that are available. The committee can save time and money if it investigates thoroughly and gets together all necessary papers and information before the organization consults an attorney.

Name: The name of the organization must be chosen carefully and included in the articles of incorporation. It cannot be the same as another corporation, nor can it be so similar to another one that it will be confusing. The words "Federal," "Reserve," "United States," "Olympic," or "Olympiad" may not be used. There are restrictions on the use of the words "bank," "trust," "trustee," and "cooperative." The commitee should check with the proper state office to see that the name is permissable. In some states, it is possible to reserve corporate names for 60 days and to submit two or three names to make certain the desired name is available.

Purpose: The purpose of an organization must be stated in the articles of incorporation. It must be lawful and, if the organization plans to apply for a tax-exemption letter from the Internal Revenue Service, it must qualify as tax-exempt. You must take extreme care that the purpose is correctly stated. For example: the word "charitable" used by itself is acceptable, but if it is used with "philanthropic" or "benevolent," it is no longer acceptable, because the words "philanthropic" and "benevolent" have no generally accepted legal meaning. This illustrates how important it is to get expert advice about incorporation.

Legal Assistance: The committee should explore all avenues of low-cost legal assistance. The librarian at the county law library can locate books for you which contain the incorporation codes of your state. In many areas senior citizens' legal aid groups will help senior citizens' associations. Law Centers, listed as nonprofit, tax-exempt corporations, can be found in the yellow pages of the telephone book. County Bar Associations have referral services and can furnish the names of attorneys specializing in corporation law.

Filing: The articles of incorporation are filed by mail with the proper state office. They must be accompanied by copies of the bylaws and the full fee. (Check the requirements of your state for the number of copies needed and the fee.)

Amendment: Articles of incorporation may be amended by sending a certificate of amendment to the proper state authority.

Chapter X

Taxes

"Do we have to pay taxes? When? What kinds? What can we do to avoid them?" are questions asked by many organizations. Exemption from federal and state income taxes, and the payment of state and city sales and property taxes are those that generally concern organizations.

Of prime importance to groups that are not organized for purposes of profit is exemption from state and federal income tax. Groups that are incorporated as nonprofit can apply to the Internal Revenue Service for exemption from federal corporate income taxes. A nonprofit association (a group that for various reasons does not want to become a corporation) can also apply for tax-exempt status, by filing the proper articles of association and bylaws with the Internal Revenue Service and filling out the required forms.

To determine whether your nonprofit organization is eligible for federal income tax exemption, obtain the Internal Revenue Service publication *How to Apply for and Retain Exempt Status for Your Organization* and Form 1023, "Application for Recognition of Exemption." A reference chart in the back of the publication lists:

1. The type of organization under which you may find your category;

2. The type of activities in which such organizations may participate to qualify as exempt;

3. Whether or not contributions deductions are allowable;

4. Under what form number you should file;

5. Whether you must file an income tax return, form 990, or some variation of it; and

6. What section of the Internal Revenue Service Code applies to your particular type of organization.

Although the chart deals with many other types of groups, we will be discussing those which come under Code 501 (c) (3) and Code 501 (c) (7).

Generally the Internal Revenue Service will issue tax-exemption letters to nonprofit organizations formed for religious, charitable, educational, and scientific research purposes. Organizations formed to foster national or international amateur sports competition, or to prevent cruelty to children or animals, may also apply. Various other groups may be eligible, but the Internal Revenue Service decides whether the organization qualifies for tax exemption. Determination is done on an individual basis.

Affiliation: If you are affiliated with an organization that is already covered by a group-exemption letter, it would automatically exempt your branch, but it must still fulfill the purposes for which the organization became exempt. Failure to comply with those purposes and restrictions can result in refusal to allow deductions for contributions, gifts, or bequests. It could endanger the status of the parent organization.

Organization are usually created to fill a need. Those that benefit the general public through education, charity, scientific research, or other helpful purposes need money to pursue their objectives. Some of the ways in which this money can be raised may be wholly dependent on whether or not the organization has tax-exempt status. For this reason, serious consideration should be given to the qualifications necessary to make your organization eligible for tax exemption.

Contributions and Grants: They are essential to the existence of an organization. Contributors will give more willingly once your tax-exempt letter has been issued. With some exceptions and limitations, contributions to an exempt organization are deductible up to 50 percent of gross income on the contributor's federal income tax returns.

QUALIFICATIONS FOR TAX-EXEMPT ELIGIBILITY

There are some general rules to follow in preparing an application for tax exemption. When you finish reading the recommendations in this chapter, make a careful study of the most recent Internal Revenue Service publications that apply to your organization. You can request them from your local Internal Revenue Service office.

Once you have determined what supporting evidence you will need to file with your application, you should gather all of the necessary information and take it to your tax accountant or your attorney for confirmation of your qualifications. The help of an expert is strongly advised in the important step of establishing your tax-exempt status.

It hardly seems necessary to emphasize that any statement in the articles of organization or bylaws that serves to act against the law would immediately eliminate any possibility of exemption, yet poorly-worded articles or bylaws may inadvertently contain such a statement. Sometimes just one word can change an entire meaning. Your attorney would be quick to observe this and suggest improved terminology. For example: purposes, according to the Internal Revenue Service, are dependent on whether or not they state *explicitly* that they are religious, educational, charitable, scientific, or for such other purposes as qualify them under Code 501 (c) (3).

An organization formed to "foster the best interests of the people" appears to fall into the categories listed above, yet the meaning is *not explicit.* To "foster the best interests of the people" is too vague. It could be accomplished in other than an exempt manner. It should state that, "The purpose of the organization is to foster the best interests of the people *only in a charitable manner,*" with provision made in the articles of organization that the purpose is restricted to the *accomplishment of this purpose only in a charitable manner.*

Social activities as expressly empowered by the articles will not sufficiently limit an organization, even if they state that it will be operated for charitable purposes. These must be backed by documentation that attests to such statements. For example: A group may form a bridge club and state in their organization document that they are a charitable club. This is not sufficiently limiting. They must state specifically just what that charity is to be. Their statement could say that the club would donate $5 out of each member's annual dues to the Crippled Children's Hospital Fund each year. Documentation would consist of cancelled checks and audited books to show the exact number of paid-up members and the correct amount donated to the Hospital.

If your organization is a women's club, a garden club, or other club under the heading of *social and recreation clubs,* you should be applying on Form 1024 under Code 501 (c) (7). The group may still be eligible for exempt status, though deductions on gifts to the organization can only be made if the organization establishes a separate charitable or scholarship fund, which must meet all the requirements listed in Code 501 (c) (3) and the related notice requirements of Section 508 (a).

If you are applying for exemption as a charitable organization, you must show that your operating purposes are beneficial to the public interest. For example: the relief of the poor, the underprivileged, or the advancement of religion, education or science. The erection and/or maintenance of public buildings and monuments or public works are examples of those purposes that are beneficial to the public interest. Lessening the burdens of government or of neighborhood tensions, the elimination of prejudice and discrimination, and the defense of human and civil rights secured by law, as well as combating community deterioration and juvenile delinquency, are all purposes considered to be worthy of exemption from some taxes.

Proof that your organization supports education must be supplied. Does your organization

1. Contribute to an existing educational institution?
2. Endow a chair?

3. Contribute to teachers' salaries?

4. Contribute to an educational institution for the explicit purpose of scientific research?

5. Award scholarships?

If your organization plans to award scholarships, then information relative to the following must be submitted:

1. What criteria is used for selecting recipients?

2. What are the rules of eligibility? They must be in the public interest.

3. By whom will the recipients be selected? Make certain judging will be impartial.

4. When a scholarship is given directly, what assurance is there that the recipient will remain in school? A scholarship given to the educational institution for the winner of such an award can be an acceptable tax deduction. The fund would be administered by the group that finances the fund, of course, but the scholarship money should be given to whatever educational institution the winner of the scholarship will attend. Rules for the awards can be made either by the group giving the scholarship or by the educational institution.

5. It will be necessary to present a copy of the scholarship application form, together with brochures and other literature describing the scholarship program.

Scientific research must be carried out in the public interest. Results of the research (including any patents, copyrights, processes, or formulae) must be made available to the public on a nondiscriminatory basis. Research can be for the United States or a state, county, or municipal government. Such research may be carried out for:

1. Obtaining scientific information that is to be published as a treatise, thesis, trade publication or in any other form that is available to the interested public;

2. Discovering a cure for a disease;

3. Aiding a community or geographical area by attracting new industry to the area, or to encourage the further development or retention of an industry if necessary;

4. Aiding in the scientific education of college or university students.

However, for exemption purposes, scientific research does not include activities incidental to commercial or industrial operations. For example: organizations engaged in the inspection or testing of materials or products, designing or construction of equipment, buildings, and other commercial enterprises can expect refusal of tax-free status.

If your group plans to engage in research, you must submit the following information:

1. An explanation of the nature of the research.

2. A brief description of research projects completed or presently engaged in.

3. How and by whom the research projects are selected.

4. Have you in the past contracted for sponsored research? If so, name the previous sponsors or grantors, the terms of the grants or contracts, and copies of the executed grants or contracts.

5. What disposition has been made, or is being made of the results of your group's research, including whether preference has or will be given to a particular organization or individual as to the results, and/or the time of release.

6. Who retains ownership or control of any patents, formulae, processes, or copyrights related to your research?

7. Include copies of publications or other media that show reports of your research activities.

Literary organizations must explain fully who benefits from their activities. Is the organization engaged in assisting writers in their work? How? Is it by offering financial assistance to struggling young writers? Or by offering them an outlet for their work? If your organization operates a book store or is engaged in publishing activities of any nature (printing, publication, or distribution of your own material or that published by others and distributed by you) include in your explanation of your activities whether sales are or will be made to the general public. Explain what type of literature is involved and how such activities relate to your stated purpose. Cancelled checks and audited books must show that money derived from sales is used for your stated purposes.

In order for organizations fostering national or international amateur sports competition to qualify for tax exemption and for the receipt of deductible contributions, no part of the activity may involve the provision of athletic facilities or equipment.

Associations devoted to the prevention of cruelty to children or animals must supply a description of the purposes and proposed activities. For example, the Internal Revenue Service would consider aiming to prevent children from working in hazardous conditions and providing protection for them an acceptable purpose. To see that laboratory animals receive high standards of care would be an acceptable purpose for a group interested in bettering those conditions.

POLITICAL ACTIVITY

Lobbying: This cannot be a substantial part of the activities of your organization. It may not influence legislation or participate in political campaigns. However, if your group chooses lobbying as one of its purposes, it must elect to do so under the provisions that allow for certain expenditures for this purpose. These can be found under "Lobbying by Public Charities," which is discussed in Part II of Chapter V in publication 557. It states that an organization (excepting churches) may elect to replace the present substantial part of the activities test with a limit defined in terms of expenditures for influencing legislation. Example: If your group wishes to lobby for better laws to control rape, it must elect to do so on Form 5678, "Election/ Revocation of Election by an Eligible Section 501 (c) (3) Organization to Make Expenditures to Influence Legislation." The form must be signed and postmarked within the first tax year to which it applies. When the form is used to revoke the election to lobby, it must also be signed and postmarked *before* the first day of the tax year to which it applies.

Communications: Sending communications to the members of your organization with regard to proposed legislation that directly affects the interests of the organization is excluded from such limits. If your organization is eligible under 501 (c) (3) and you have elected to be subject to the limitations on lobbying expenditures, you must use Part VI of schedule A (form 990) to compute these limitations.

According to the Internal Revenue Service, lobbying to influence legislation, for purposes of this provision, means: Any attempt to influence any legislation through a move to affect the opinions of the general public or any segment of it; and any attempt to influence legislation through communication with any member or employee of a legislative body, or with any government official or employee who may participate in the formulation of the legislation.

In response to a written request by a governmental body, committee, or other subdivision, the organization may provide technical advice or assistance. Giving such advice without a request would constitute influencing legislation. However, it is possible to make available the results of nonpartisan analysis, study, or research.

Communication with any legislative body that might affect the existence of the organization, its powers and duties, its tax-exempt status, or the deduction of contributions to the organization would not in itself constitute influencing legislation and is therefore within the rights of the organization.

Limitations on Lobbying: The Internal Revenue Service imposes limitations on the amount an organization can spend on lobbying. This is a percentage of the organization's "exempt purpose expenditures." Your group should check with the Internal Revenue Service for its latest rulings.

Exempt Purpose Expenditures: Those expenditures that an organization incurs in the accomplishment of its exempt purposes. They include:

1. Administrative expenses paid or incurred for the exempt purposes of the organization.

2. Under the lobbying election, expenditures for the purpose of influencing legislation.

Election to come under the lobbying provision will remain in effect for all tax years until revoked by the organization. It is advisable to seek further information on this from your Internal Revenue Service office.

OTHER FACTORS TO CONSIDER

Exempt Status: It should be applied for as soon after formation as possible. It must be made within 15 months of the date of organization. Before filing, it is necessary that you determine whether or not you could be classified as a private foundation. If not, you should notify the Internal Revenue Service of this fact in writing.

Dissolution Requirements: Processing your application can be more rapidly accomplished if your articles of organization provide for insuring permanent dedication of assets for exempt purposes. Even though reliance may be placed on your state's laws to establish this, the articles still must comply with Internal Revenue Service rulings.

1. The articles must clearly state that, upon dissolution, the assets are to be distributed to a like exempt organization; or

2. They may state that at dissolution the assets shall be given to the federal, state, or local government to be used for a public purpose; or

3. If a beneficiary is to be awarded the assets, it must be one that qualifies as exempt according to Internal Revenue Service rules. Since the beneficiary organization may not be qualified, no longer in existence, unwilling or unable to accept these assets, provision for the distribution of assets as described in paragraphs one and two should also be included.

4. Your articles of organization may not authorize the distribution of assets to any individual or shareholder. However, it should authorize the payment of all bills and indebtedness prior to distribution on dissolution.

Purpose Requirements: Limitations as to the purposes of the organization that appear *only in the bylaws* or other rules *do not* satisfy the requirements of the Internal Revenue Service. These powers and purposes must be clearly defined in the *articles of organization.*

Interpretation of an organization's articles is controlled by the laws of the state in which the organization is formed. Because the laws vary among states, the terms of the articles may have a different meaning under state law than the generally accepted meaning. When this happens, it is necessary that a clear, convincing reference is established either by relevant court decisions or other appropriate state authorities before acceptance by the Internal Revenue Service. For example: When the articles of organization state that it is *benevolent* and/or *philanthropic,* it is generally accepted by the public to mean that it is *charitable.* However, they do not have the same accepted legal meaning, and under the laws of the state may permit activities that are broader than the word *charitable* as intended by the Internal Revenue Service on tax exemptions.

If the group owns real estate and has income from it or has other like assets, discuss the situation with your tax accountant or attorney before you apply, to be sure it does not affect your status.

HOW TO APPLY FOR RECOGNITION OF EXEMPTION

If your purposes make you eligible to apply for tax-exempt status, you will need to gather together certain items necessary for the completion of "Application for Recognition of Exemption," Form 1023, Section 501 (c) (3).

1. Official full name of the organization. (Have you checked to be sure that it is not the same or similar to another in your area?)

2. Your employer identification number. If you do not have one, you must fill out and attach Form SS-4. This is available at the Internal Revenue Service office and is a requirement even if you have no employees.

3. The principal address of your organization.

4. The box 501 (e) applies to cooperative hospital services. 501 (f) applies to cooperative educational services. If you are under either of these check that box.

5. You need to know the month your annual accounting ends.

6. What is the date that your organization was first formed and/or incorporated?

7. Activity codes are listed in the back of your application form. Find the three closest to the activities of your organization.

8. Has the organization filed federal income tax? If so, state the form, the numbers and years filed as well as the Internal Revenue Service office in which you filed.

9. Has your organization filed exempt organization information returns? If so, state the form numbers, years filed, and the office where filed. Attach copies.

Part II: In this part of the application, you will be asked to check the type of organizing and operating documents and to attach conformed copies of these. Be sure your attorney has checked these documents before you send them in with your application, to be certain they will qualify. If your group is a nonprofit corporation (or an unincorporated organization with articles of association and by-laws), you must include a signed copy of the bylaws.

Part III: Here you are asked to attach representative copies of solicitations for financial support, as well as to give information about other earnings.

Section 2, requires that you attach details of all fund-raising activities, selective mailings, etc., in describing the organization's fund-raising program.

Section 3 asks for a narrative description of all of your activities, without using the language of the documents. Although the same information is required, tell about it in a more detailed fashion and in your own words. Information for Section 3 of part three can be found in your minutes book. Much of the information asked for in sections 4a, b, c, d, e, and f can also be found in your minutes book.

Section 5 is self explanatory.

Section 6 may require copies of reports if your organization is financially accountable to another organization.

Section 7a and b, and Section 8 are self explanatory.

Section 9: You need substantiating evidence of how the recipients or beneficiaries will be chosen.

Section 10a requires a schedule of membership fees and dues to be attached. Refer to your bylaws.

Section 10b attachment must be a copy of promotional literature to attract members. (Brochures, mailers, etc.)

Section 11: You may wish to file Form 5678, if you will be engaged in activities to influence legislation as explained earlier.

Section 13: If you claim Section 508a does not apply to you, you will need to attach an explanation of your basis for the claim that you are not a lodge paying benefits to members for sickness, accident, etc., unless it is for charitable purposes.

Part IV: If you are setting up a private foundation, see your attorney and/or your tax accountant before filing for your tax exemption. Your attorney and accountant can take into consideration all the needs of the foundation and advise you as to the best procedures for filing your application.

Part V: You will need your financial statements taken from the treasurer's books, and perhaps some information from your minutes book, to make out the schedules called for and which must be attached. These include:

1. Detailed statement of receipts and expenditures for the current year.

2. Income sources, fully explained.

3. Disbursements must be itemized, and, where necessary, an explanation must be made of the reason for the disbursement.

4. Bank statements, ledger sheets, profit and loss or other similar statements are not sufficient by themselves.

5. Administrative and general operating expenses must be kept separate from expenditures made directly in the furtherance of the purposes for which the organization filed for exemption.

6. Balance sheet for the current year, and three immediate prior years, (or if less than three years, for the years that the organization has been in existence) is required.

7. Financial data for the period ending 60 days prior to the date of application must be submitted, if the current year is less than a full year.

Part VI: If your organization plans to give scholarships, complete Schedule B and attach sample application form. If your organization intends to promote amateur sports competition, complete Schedule G.

GETTING LEGAL HELP

Your organization may have different requirements than those already listed. To be sure what they are, see your attorney. Take with you all of the information already listed, and fill out the application with his help. You will save time and money, and accomplish your purpose.

Before reviewing the application with your attorney, check carefully to see that you have completed all the necessary information, that you have all the documents needed to be attached to the application. Be sure that the name of the organization and address, as well as the phone number, appears at the top of each sheet of the attachments. If the organization does not have a principal office, give the name and address of an officer to be contacted.

When everything has been reviewed and is in the proper form, be sure that the application is signed by the appropriate officers.

Mail the completed application and attachments to the proper Key District Director (see list that follows), who will either refer the case to the National Office for issuance of a Ruling, issue a favorable Determination Letter, or issue a proposed Adverse Determination Letter denying the exempt status claimed in the application.

KEY DISTRICT DIRECTORS

IF PRINCIPAL OFFICE IS IN ONE OF THESE DISTRICTS	SEND APPLICATION TO: DISTRICT DIRECTOR FOR KEY DISTRICT INTERNAL REVENUE SERVICE
Atlanta, Greensboro, Columbia, Nashville	EP/EO Division, P.O. Box 632 Atlanta, Georgia, 30301

Austin, Cheyenne, Denver, Albuquerque, New Orleans	EP/EO Division, P.O. Box 2135 Austin, Texas 78767
Baltimore, District of Columbia, Pittsburgh, Richmond, any U.S. possession or foreign country.	EP/EO Division, P.O. Box 13163 Technical & Service Staff Baltimore, Md. 21203
Boston, Burlington, Portsmouth, Augusta, Hartford, Providence	EP/EO Division, P.O. Box 9081 JFK Post Office Boston, Mass. 02203
Brooklyn, Albany, Buffalo	EP/EO Division, P.O. Box 1680 General Post Office Brooklyn, N.Y. 11202
Chicago	EP/EO Division, P.O. Box A-3617 Chicago, Ill. 60690
Cincinnati, Indianapolis, Louisville	EP/EO Division, P.O. Box 2508 Cincinnati, Ohio, 45201
Cleveland, Parkersburg	EP/EO Division, P.O. Box 99187 Cleveland, Ohio 44199
Dallas, Little Rock, Oklahoma City, Wichita	EO2 Code 309, 1100 Commerce St. Dallas, Texas 75242
Jacksonville, Birmingham, Jackson	EP/EO Division, P.O. Box 35045 Jacksonville, Fla. 32202
Los Angeles, Honolulu, Phoenix	EP/EO Division, P.O. Box 2350 Los Angeles, Ca. 90053
Manhattan	EP/EO Division, P.O. Box 3200 Church Street Station New York, N.Y. 10008

Newark	EP/EO Division, P.O. Box 260 Newark, N.J. 07101
Philadelphia, Wilmington	EP/EO Division, P.O. Box 12821 Philadelphia, Pa. 19106
San Francisco, Reno, Salt Lake City	EP/EO Division, P.O. Box 36001 450 Golden Gate Ave., San Francisco, Ca. 94102
Seattle, Anchorage, Boise, Helena, Portland	EP/EO Division, P.O. Box 21224 Seattle, Wash. 98111
St. Louis, Des Moines, Omaha, Springfield	EP/EO Division, Group 7206, P.O. Box 1123, Central Station St. Louis, Mo. 63188
St. Paul, Aberdeen, Fargo, Milwaukee	EP/EO Division, Group 1902 316 No. Robert St., St. Paul, Minn. 55101

PROCESSING OF APPLICATIONS

Incomplete Applications: They should be returned to the applicant along with a letter of explanation. There will be no further consideration until the corrected application is resubmitted. The time period for resubmission will be given in the letter of explanation.

Appeal of Adverse Determination Letter: This may be made through the Key District Office to the Regional Director of Appeals within 30 days from the date of the Adverse Determination Letter. If no appeal is filed within the 30-day period, the proposed Adverse Determination Letter is final.

Regional Office Appeal: It should contain the following:
1. Organization's name, address, and Employer Identification Number.

2. A statement that the organization wishes to appeal the Determination.

3. The date and symbols on the Determination Letter.

4. A statement of facts supporting the organization's position in any contested factual issue.

5. State what law or other authority the organization is relying on in support of the stated facts.

6. State if the organization desires a conference.

The Statement of Facts: (item 4) This must be declared true under penalties of perjury. The following signed declaration must accompany the appeal: "Under penalties of perjury, I declare that I have examined the statements of facts presented in this appeal, and in any accompanying schedules and statements, and to the best of my knowledge and belief, it is true, correct, and complete." This should be signed by a principal officer who represents the organization. This could be the president, the vice president, or the treasurer of the organization. Representation may also be by an attorney, a certified public accountant, or an individual enrolled to practice before the Internal Revenue Service. When the organization is represented by one or more of these without the principal officer, they must have with them a *Power of Attorney* so that they can sign in place of the principal officer.

Information: Any information forwarded to the Internal Revenue Service may be used in subsequent examination of your organization's returns.

No Return: Application material cannot be expected to be returned. Send only photocopies of all attachments and documents.

ISSUANCE OF EXEMPTION LETTER

Effective Date of Exemption: This date is as of the date of the formation of the organization, if, during the period prior to the date of the Ruling or Determination Letter, the purposes and activities were those as required by law. If the organization is required to alter the activities or substantially amend the articles of organization to qualify for the Ruling or Determination Letter, the exemption will be effective only as of the date specified in the Ruling.

Tax Refund: Upon obtaining recognition of exemption, the organization may file a claim for refund of income tax paid for the period for which the exempt status is recognized.

OTHER TAXES

Once you have become tax-exempt, you must still pay some other taxes and fill out some forms for those taxes from which you are exempt. Exemption from federal income tax does not preclude paying other federal, state, county, and local taxes. Your Internal Revenue Service office has pamphlets that will help you determine what taxes you are responsible for, and how to pay them.

Federal Tax Form 990: Return of organization exempt from income tax: This must be filed on or before the 15th day of the 5th month after the end of your accounting period. Example: If your fiscal year ends May 31st, you must file on or before October 15th.

Federal Tax Form: This 990T must be filed if you have a gross income of $10,000 or more from business unrelated to and not directly applicable to the exempt purposes of your organization.

Social Security: As a tax-exempt organzation, you may elect (with your employees' agreement) to have your employees covered by Social Security. (See Publication 15, Supplement SS15, and 15A of the Internal Revenue Service for particulars.) Social Security must be paid promptly, to avoid confusion and penalties.

Withholding Exemptions: Every employee must sign Form W4 when starting to work. Withholding, FICA taxes, or both must be filed quarterly by employers on Form 941. Organizations reporting on withheld income must file on Form 941E.

Part-Time Help: Keep records of hourly wages for part-time.

W2 Forms must be filled out and given to each employee by January 31st of the following year. No later than February 28th, send copy A of all W2 forms issued for the previous year to the Social Security Adminstration.

Earned Income Credit refers only to advances made to low-income people who are in the employ of the organization. The taxpayer's expected earned and adjusted gross income must both be less than $10,000, to be eligible for such advances. It is recommended that the Employer's Tax Guide be studied in order to properly compute the advance payment of EIC and to file the proper returns. Copies can be obtained from your IRS office.

Keep four years of records of advance earned Income Credit (EIC) payments for possible Internal Revenue Service review. Records must include:
1. Copies of Form W-5.
2. Amounts and dates of all wage and advance EIC.
3. Dates of each employee's employment.
4. Dates and amounts of tax deposits made.
5. Copies of returns you have filed.

W-3: By February 28th, withholding forms must include Copy A of all W-2 forms and those you gave employees for the year before.

Federal Unemployment Tax: Organizations holding a 501 (c) (3) exemption are exempt from payment of this tax. After you have received your exemption, check to see if you are listed in the *Cumulative List of Organizations* published by the Treasury Department, to be sure your exempt status is recognized. A copy can be obtained from your Internal Revenue Service office.

State Income Tax Laws: These vary, so you should check with the proper tax authority regarding application for exemption.

State Sales Taxes: They must be paid unless the organization applies to the proper authority for a sales number which exempts the organization from the sales tax. The organization is responsible for collecting the sales tax on any merchandise it sells and must send it to the proper state authority with a report, usually on a quarterly basis.

Property Taxes: If applicable, they must be paid promptly to avoid penalites. If you lease, check to be sure you are not expected to pay the taxes on the property.

Each city, county, and state operates differently to collect taxes, and even as to what taxes are collected. It is important that the organization learns what taxes it is responsible for and pays these taxes promptly. Changes in tax rulings should be checked, and advice from a tax account or an attorney is recommended.

Chapter XI

Finances

"Money is the name of the game" is an expression heard often today. It is true that money is the final ingredient necessary to the success of any enterprise, whether for a business venture or a charitable mission.

Membership dues account for a percentage of the money organizations need to reach their goals, but dues are rarely enough. The organization must reach out for other help. Members are urged to contribute to the cause in many ways. One is through endowment funds.

ENDOWMENT FUNDS

Members and friends are asked to give gifts in memory of loved ones, to honor one or more individuals, or to commemorate a special occasion, in order to raise money for a particular purpose. These funds are self perpetuating. Only the interest from them may be used, and that only for the purpose for which it was designated at the time of formation. Funds should be invested in federally guaranteed, interest-bearing securities at the highest rate available for long-term investment. Members are encouraged to contribute to the fund through reminders in the house organ and newsletters.

Endowment Book: To encourage members to give to the fund, you can design a special endowment book, permanently and attractively bound, in which the names of donors and those honored can be inscribed. Whole pages or even sections can be devoted to large donors as a special inducement for additional contributions. The book should be on display at all meetings. Other funds are developed differently.

BUILDING FUND

A building fund was started by a member of an organization when it was realized that the headquarters would soon need repairs. The slogan for the fund had an original twist: "Why not own a piece of the building that serves as your organization's headquarters. Buy a brick for $10. Buy two for $20. Each brick represents your personal interest in your organization. Buy a brick!"

Bricks covered in embroidered cloth, which could be used as door stops, were offered to those who gave more than $100. The bricks were made up by the members of the committee entrusted with promoting the fund.

BEQUESTS

Suggestions can be made that members make a gift to the organization in their wills.

SCHOLARSHIP FUNDS

Purpose: Your organization may want to establish a scholarship fund as one of its qualifications for tax exemption. Interest and increased membership in the organization can be stimulated if scholarships are awarded in fields linked to its objectives.

How to Get Donations:

1. Send out letters or brochures, in which the benefits to both the donor and the winner of the scholarship are outlined.

2. Arrange a meeting of potential donors, at which time a speaker can elaborate on the needs that can be met by contributions to the fund.

3. When possible, the sponsoring organization should lend financial support to the scholarship fund.

Contributions: Any contributions to the fund should be set up as a restricted endowment fund (self-perpetuating trust), with only the interest used for the awards, unless the donor indicates otherwise. Such funds may not be used for any other purpose than the one for which it has been designated. As an example: "This scholarship is for the woman over the age of 35, in need of financial assistance to enable her to resume studies, which would make it possible for her to reenter the business world." Another example might be: "For the college student who has his master's degree, but needs financial aid to complete his doctorate." Some organizations might wish to give scholarships to high school seniors to help them with tuition to college.

GRANTS

These can be a good source of support for certain types of projects. Investigate the possibilities of getting a grant for your purposes through the resources of your public library. There you will find factual information to help you.

The *Foundation Directory* contains lists of foundations. It gives the name, address, date of incorporation, the names of the donors, what purpose or purposes the grants support, and if the grants are only available in certain areas or specific locations. Financial data about assets, gifts, expenditures, and the amounts for each grant as well as the number of grants given in a stated number of years is included. You will find the names of officers, trustees, or directors there too.

The Foundation Center has headquarters at 888 Seventh Avenue, New York, N.Y. 10019. If you need information that you were unable to find in the *Foundation Directory*, you can inquire about its other facilities, which have information available on microfilm and cards. The center has three national libraries located in New York, Washington, D.C., and Chicago. In addition, there are 50 regional libraries throughout the country. These are subunits of independent public, college, and foundation libraries. Use of the libraries is free. Charges are made only for photocopying material.

Space does not permit the listing of all the material available to the grant-seeker. There are many books written on the subject. Two that give useful sources of information are *The Art of Winning Foundation Grants* by Howard Hillman and Karin Abarbanel, and *The Art of Winning Government Grants* by Howard Hillman, both published by Vanguard Press, Inc. 424 Madison Avenue, New York, N.Y. 10017.

OBTAINING MATCHING FUNDS

Let us suppose that your organization's purpose is to alleviate hunger in undeveloped parts of the world. You have made a proposal to a foundation for a grant to be used for a pilot project. You are to research the possibilities of finding water in a arid land, devising an irrigation system when you find the water, and ultimately learning what kind of food production could be developed, using a certain type of farm equipment.

The foundation is willing to give you the grant, but only under certain conditions. The principal condition is that, after the research has been completed, the project should be funded by other sources and continued in operation until it is certain that the people in the area can raise sufficient food for their needs through the use of irrigation.

It is imperative that you get another source for the funds to meet these requirements. How?

Direct Solicitation: This may be your answer. It will require some time and research. Although you undoubtedly did much research in making up your grant proposal, you will find there are some different resources available to you in this task. But first we need to take another look at your purposes.

Purposes: Your purposes have been defined in your proposal for a grant, but now you are going beyond the experimental pilot project. You must consider all the varied conditions, both positive and negative, involved in making the experiment work permanently. Redefine your purposes. Do it on paper. When you think it is ready for presentation, tape it and listen to it carefully. Would you find it worthy of a large investment if you were the donor?

Goals: Your goals should be reexamined in the light of this future projection. Let us determine that we must:

1. Find water, or we cannot go on with the project. It is of prime importance to our final goals. Has every possibility been researched geologically, to determine whether there is some probability of locating a source of water?

2. Estimate the cost of materials, labor, and expertise to bring the water to the designated area. How much time must you allow for this?

3. Now ascertain the amount of irrigation required to produce a sufficient supply of food needed for X number of people.

4. Supply the project with machinery, soil conditioners, fertilizers, and seed before the proposed project can be assessed. In what quantities do we need them?

5. Educate the population of that area in the use of tools and materials to produce food.

In addition to the statistics you have just now reevaluated, you will need to do some research on the organizations you may be contacting for contributions. In seeking organizations that might have some relation, directly or indirectly, to your project, you will be looking for the following possibilities:

1. A firm dealing in drilling for water wells.

2. A manufacturer of farming machinery.

3. A company dealing in soil conditioners and in fertilizers.

4. A seed company interested in promoting new seeds.

5. An airline company, since you will be moving some specially trained people to your project's location.

6. A shipping line that could be involved in moving the equipment to your project.

7. Someone interested in agricultural development in the middle-eastern countries.

You will uncover other possibilities as you go along.

It will be necessary to study the information about:

1. Financial status, profits and possible tax needs.

2. Management.

3. Products, and how they can be used for your project.

4. Other activities that may be helpful.

5. The proper person to contact.

Sources for this information can be found in directories, books on financial analysis, almanacs, annual report files, etc. You can find most of these in your public library. Among the best are: *Standard Industrial Classification Manual,* issued by the executive office of the president, office of management and budget. It is made up of divisions of statistical policy. It defines industries and covers the entire field of economic activities. You will find S.I.C. classifications under a numerical index of major groups of industry, groups and industries of manufacturing and agriculture, etc.

Standard and Poor's Register of Corporations, Directors and Executive Indexes has the S.I.C. index in Section I, so you can quickly determine the line of business you are seeking by the use of the appropriate S.I.C. code number. The *Register* lists the following information on companies: chairman of the board, and chairman of the executive committee, the president and the chief executive officer, senior vice-president and sometimes others, treasurer, division presidents and vice-presidents of office, buying, or foreign subsidiaries. It may also list the sales manager and advertising manager. It may mention other directors. It gives the name of the primary bank, the primary law firm, the number of employees, and its products or activities. It reports on accounts, sales range, and other information where necessary. To bring changes up-to-date, *Standard and Poor's* issues a monthly supplement found in the library.

The Directory of Corporate Affiliations lists the parent company and those functioning under it. For example: A newspaper syndicate owning papers in many cities, or a tobacco company with subsidiaries in many states. It is published by the National Register Publishing Company, Inc.

The World Marketing Directory, published by Dun and Bradstreet, lists principal international business under nations. It gives the name, address, cable telex number, S.I.C. number, sales, products, employees, and also whether they import or export, or both.

Reference Book of Corporate Management, also published by Dun and Bradstreet, gives the names and positions, past and present, held with the company, education and specialized training, and where applicable, service in the armed forces. The names are listed alphabetically under the title of the corporation.

Million Dollar Directory, published by Dun and Bradstreet, lists in Volume I major businesses with a net worth of $1,000,000. Volume 2 lists those worth between $500,000 and $999,000. It includes domestic subsidiaries of foreign firms.

Moodys Industrial Manual gives complete reports on the history, acquisitions, subsidiaries, affiliates, and such things as recapitalization, business and properties (including, where applicable, marine operations), sources of revenue and how much, as well as sources of pretax income in dollars (by the million). It lists management, officers, trustees, auditors, shareholder relations, trustee meetings, annual meetings, the number of stockholders and employees. Listed also are the general office, income account, gross income and net income returned to earnings. It lists the registrar, dividend disbursement, and transfer agent. It shows if it is listed on the New York Stock Exchange, or others.

In addition to these, there are books on government statistics, European financial almanacs, and financial analysis. You will find books like *The Language of Money, A to Z Finance,* and others that will help you.

There are value line surveys that give information on whether industries as a group, or as a whole, are now doing poorly or well, or that there is some growth anticipated. Annual reports of individual corporations can be seen for research. They are arranged in alphabetical files in the reference rooms of most large libraries. Business laws of your state should be checked to see if there is reference to any part of your project. Be sure to see your attorney and/or your tax accountant before you complete any negotiations.

Now, if you have done your homework, you should be armed with the information you need to ask for and get the money you will require for the completion of your project.

Before you begin to write your letter, you will want to define:

1. What you have learned from your research about the corporation that makes it probable that it would be interested in what you propose.

2. What part of the whole would be of special interest to it.

3. What possible return can you offer it that would increase its interest. Money? Tax deductions? How much can you estimate when you know the net profit? Often the financial statements show large profits.

4. What influence its previous contributions would have on whether or not it would consider supporting your project.

5. What affect any restriction it may make would have on your proposal.

You should learn who is the final authority for approval of the contribution and what office that person holds. Before you write your letter, you will want to know some things about this person's life style: clubs, particular sports and cultural interests, and other activities that could make communication easier for both the letter you write and in the follow-up conference you expect to have with the prospective contributor.

Marquis Who's Who in America, published by A.N. Marquis Company, 200 East Ohio Street, Chicago, Illinois 60611, is the place to find the information you need. It lists about 70,000 leaders in all fields of endeavor.

Your letter should be sincere in tone, state facts that appeal to the interests of the person you hope will become a contributor to your project, and ask for a specified meeting date.

SAMPLE LETTER

Mr. John Doe, President
Old Mill Flour Company,
Anytown, U.S.A. 00000

Dear Mr. Doe,

"Bread is the staff of life." Since bread is made of flour, your company is in the business of maintaining life.

Flour is used to make pancakes for the breakfast of millions of people all over the world. You supply much of it. Yet there are those who have no flour for pancakes or bread—not for breakfast or any other meal. They are hungry! They are starving! You answer, "Feed them." We feed them, but tomorrow they are hungry again.

World Opportunity, a nonprofit corporation, has plans for a pilot project to assist these people. Funding is available from the Blank Foundation, but matching funds and help are needed.

Irrigating systems, farming machinery, seed for grain, fertilizers, and teachers are needed to help these people help themselves. They need to grow their own food. Your experience and knowledge of grains, so essential to the success of this project, can mean a great deal.

Please call me at Grant 1–2345. Let's talk more about this over lunch.

Very truly yours,

The letter is the first step in your campaign for funds. When you meet over lunch, you must be fortified with all the information you have researched. You will know how to greet Mr. Doe, make him feel comfortable with some conversation about his favorite activity, and lead into the facts relating to your proposal for financial help.

If the man does not call you, you can follow with a second letter.

This time you will want to go a little further into the ways in which his knowledge will be useful and give some factual reasons why he should be interested in your project. You might conclude with mentioning that, since you feel his company probably is interested in saving some money on taxes, you would be happy to meet with him to discuss the possibilities.

Letters for such projects could be sent to drilling companies, to people in the business of laying out irrigation systems, to the manufacturers of farm equipment and others, using the same general technique. Don't expect 100 percent results, but then you really only need a few large contributors.

DIRECT CONTRIBUTIONS

Maybe your project does not qualify for a grant, or need the substantial amounts we were just discussing, but you do need money to go on with the purposes of your group. One way is to ask for direct contributions.

Everyone receives letters that start with "Dear Friend, We need your contribution to help with . . ." Most of these letters land in the trash basket. After all, one can give to only a few at best.

If you want your letter to be saved from the trash basket, you should know to whom you must send your request, and what the possibilities may be that you will receive the amount of money you require. Sometimes you may have to get contributions from many sources to make up the whole amount you need. You will need to know something about the people and companies to find out which ones have interests compatible with your project. Knowing this, you can devise a "hook" to get the attention of your reader.

Your letter needs to have eye appeal. It should stand out from the junk mail received every day.

One letter that attracted our attention wasn't a letter at all. It began immediately to tell a fascinating, though short, bit of history that seemingly had nothing to do with the purpose of the mailing. In fact, at the end, it stated that you were not to consider this as a solicitation. Does that seem contrary to what was needed? Not at all.

It was part of a planned campaign to get attention. It was soon followed by another letter that again was not a letter, but went a little further into the history. It was cleverly written, because now you began to relate to the people in the history. The buildup had begun. It was not many pieces of mail later that the request for financial help was made. By that time you were involved with the history, and the project as a whole, and could hardly refuse. Too much trouble? Not when you must compete with the many groups that solicit money.

You must be original. You must be creative. But that is not enough. You need to know exactly what you are going to say to your prospective contributor.

1. Get all the important facts and figures together.

2. Ask yourself all the questions that might arise.

3. Make certain that you have all the answers.

4. Can you relate the contributor's activities to your project as a means of arousing interest?

5. Have you researched to discover in what ways you can suggest that the contributor will benefit? A plaque on the door of a donated hospital room, or even just the self-esteem that comes from doing a charitable or public service, and, of course, the tax deductions.

6. Can you give at least five good reasons why the potential contributor should consider your project rather than others equally worthwhile?

When you have evaluated all the facts and figures you have assembled, you will have a fair idea of the number of letters you will have to send out. You will be fortunate if 5 percent respond, but don't give up. Remember, we said only a few letters elude the wastebasket. If you want to save your letter from that fate, you will slant it toward the interests of the person or company you are addressing. You will need to give some facts about your project. Your letter needs to be so appealing that the contributor can hardly refuse.

Before you start to write, it may pay you to read some of *America's Most Successful Fund-Raising Letters,* put out by Public Service Materials Center and edited by Joseph Dermer. Your local library probably has it or can get it for you.

For example, maybe you need additional funds for the halfway house your group has been sponsoring. You know funds are more difficult to obtain each year. What can you write that will create enough concern to get you the needed money?

SAMPLE LETTER

Dear Mrs . . .

When you were a youngster, the streets and parks were safe. This is no longer true; for many of today's young women, leaving home is a traumatic experience. Many have been approached. Many have been raped. Some have come to us for haven because a close relative has raped them and they are afraid to tell the family about it. They need a place of safety. They need understanding of the situation in which they have been placed, through no fault of their own. Here at Haven Halfway House for runaway or pregnant girls, we provide a climate for their rehabilitation.

The police bring girls to us—runaways—many of them dazed and horrified by their experiences. We comfort them and see that they are given proper emotional and, when necessary, medical care. Some girls want to keep their babies and need to learn how to care for them. In all cases, we try to erase the inevitable scars left by their experience.

Those that are still of school age are given proper schooling. Those old enough are trained so they can earn a living. Then we help them to get jobs.

We extend to you an invitation to visit our home to see how contributions from people like you have helped make life meaningful for these girls.

It will be a pleasure to take you on a tour of our premises at . . . Street, just a short distance from your home. You will be pleasantly surprised to learn how far as little as $100 can go in bringing comfortable quarters, physical and emotional help for these young women, any one of which might have been saved from their plight if they had had the safety of a home like yours.

Your tax-deductible gift will be welcomed, indeed. Thank you from the girls and myself.

Sincerely,

In the event that you feel you need the advice and help of professional fund-raisers, you should consider that the cost is great. You must pay for the professional help, no matter how much or little you finally end up making. The expense should be watched. Fund-raisers tend to spend large sums for brochures printed on heavy paper and huge mailings. It is possible that you could accomplish the same final results with a good task force and some ingenuity. (See "Fund Raising," Chapter XV.)

Financial Points to Remember:

1. In all situations that have to do with the finances of the organization, you need people with a sense of responsibility and dedication to your cause.

2. Be sure that the people handling large sums of money are bonded.

3. See to it that checks are always made out to your organization, not to any individual.

4. Receipts must be made up in triplicate. One goes to the donor, one goes to the treasurer, and one is kept by the member soliciting the donation.

Chapter XII

Contracts, Insurance, and Permits

Eventually every organization will face the need to sign a contract. When an organization engages a program or speaker, plans an exhibit, or has work done on the headquarters, some detailed form of agreement must be made. Such an agreement is a contract to do or not to do a certain thing. It is enforceable through legal action.

With a written contract, misunderstandings, disappointments, and legal problems can be avoided. The contract serves as a reminder to both parties of exactly what has been agreed upon, thus no one has to rely upon memory.

Before an agreement that will result in a contract is reached, the president of the organization, the executive board, or the appropriate chairperson generally investigates three or more places to hold the function or asks several companies or contractors to bid. During these preliminary negotiations, the organization determines which place or company will meet its needs best. The terms can be agreed upon orally. Such negotiations ordinarily result in a binding contract, when it is understood that a written contract embodying the terms already agreed upon will be signed at a predetermined time.

Essentials of Contracts:

1. They must be written in proper contract form. Never consider an implied agreement.

117

2. Any changes written into the contract after it is typed must be initialed by both parties.

3. Whether the contract is for space for meetings or for other needs, details of exact requirements: fees, stated dates and times for starting and ending the contract, as well as performance and completion, must be included before the contract is signed by both parties.

4. Exceptions are banks and some public organizations, which frequently make oral agreements for meeting rooms. The date should be put on their calendar as you watch. Banks often offer use of their rooms gratis. Other public places may charge a small rental fee.

Rental Contracts: If the organization rents space for a function such as a sale, exhibit, luncheon, or program, the following list must be checked carefully before signing the contract to make sure that everything needed is adequate and in good working order. Take the list with you and check each item as *poor, fair, good,* or *excellent* as a means of evaluation.

1. Parking rules should be investigated and, when it is necessary, inquire of the police department if you may have special tags that permit parking in no-parking zones for a limited period of time. You may have to get special permission for loading and unloading. Be sure you know how to get into the parking area. If it is locked, find out who has the key and how to contact that person to either open the facility or give you the key.

2. Proper ventilation is a must. If there are air conditioners, make sure that they are in good working order.

3. Restroom facilities should be investigated, to be sure that they are adequate. Make a note of the location in relation to the meeting room you will be using.

4. Kitchen equipment must be inspected if you will be using it. Check the rules for using the equipment. List any extraordinary needs or items missing in the kitchen in the contract.

5. Tables, chairs, podium, etc., should be seen, to determine if they are sturdy and safe to use. Make sure the required number is available. Supply the person who will set them up with a diagram for seating. Be certain there is ample space for your audience.

6. Stage and other equipment should be checked, to see if they are adequate for the program planned. For a performance, actors will need a dressing room.

7. Acoustics should be good enough for your speaker to be heard distinctly. All sound equipment should be in working condition.

Verification that everything is satisfactory should be made, and the contract signed *only* when it includes the following:

1. Agreement to occupy the designated space at a specified time. Include a diagram of the room or rooms you will be occupying with their names or numbers.

2. The rental fee for the specified period of time. Be sure you know if you must pay a maintenance man separately to clean up after the meeting or if it is included in the rental.

3. A list of all the items and equipment you want included in the rental.

4. If there is to be a deposit, is it to be refunded at termination of the contract or used as credit against the rental?

5. If there is a possibility of cancellation, what is the deadline? What is the penalty for cancellation after deadline?

6. Who is responsible for accidental damage to the building or equipment?

Office Space Rental: This is usually in the form of a lease. A standard form includes the basic necessary terms and space for requirements of both parties. The penalty for cancellation should be included.

Agreements: Agreements with speakers frequently are made orally. A letter of confirmation requiring an affirmative reply should follow. In essence this constitutes a contract. (See "Duties of the Other Officers," Chapter V.)

Employee Contracts: If the organization employs office help, contracts avoid much misunderstanding. The contract should state the salary, intervals of payment, hours required each week, hours required each day, and starting and ending times. If there will be overtime work, the contract should include the rate of payment. For a permanent office worker, some written arrangement for vacation or holiday time should go into the agreement, so that the worker does not expect something the organization is not prepared to give. Percentage and time of salary increases can be included. The same type of agreement is effective for temporary help. It should describe the work to be accomplished.

Contracts for Repairs or Construction: If your organization is planning major repairs or construction of a building, be sure to get bids from three licensed contractors and legal advice before signing a contract. The contract should specify what is to be done, what material is to be used, and the quality of workmanship. The completion date and the penalty for incompletion beyond a named date should be included. Codes, permits, possible liens, energy requirements, and many other items must be considered in such contracts. Investigate thoroughly and get expert advice before signing anything.

Service Contracts: If the organization owns a building or rents office space, it may want to contract for regular service for equipment maintenance or heating oil. The contract should be read carefully before signing, to be certain it gives the specific services you require at the times you need them. It should state any additional costs for parts and extra calls and whether the service is automatic or only on call.

A service contract calendar should be maintained by the recording secretary. The regular times of service are listed and checked off when done. When extra calls are made or parts replaced, the cost and date should be entered. This gives a record of performance that is valuable when the time comes for service renewal or equipment replacement.

Insurance: Discuss with your insurance agent the types of insurance that will cover the needs of your organization. If you own property, you will probably want to carry policies to cover theft, fire, and liability. If your organization engages in fund-raising, you may want to take out a blanket policy to cover the event. Volunteer workers who use their cars in carrying out their duties must have automobile insurance. Investigate what coverage is needed to protect your employees.

Postal Permits: Nonprofit tax-exempt organizations can apply at local post offices for a nonprofit bulk-rate mailing permit. Fees and special rates for nonprofit organizations can be obtained from the postmaster. To apply you need to bring with you supporting evidence of your exempt status. This includes copies of the exemption issued by the Internal Revenue Service, your articles of incorporation or charter, constitution, and bylaws. You will also need samples of bulletins and programs that are qualifying proof of the organization's nonprofit activities.

Upon approval of your application by postal authorities, you will be given publications which contain complete information on mailings.

Other Permits: Depending upon your area, permits may be required for fund-raising activities, the sale of food or alcoholic beverages. Check with local authorities.

Special Points to Remember:

1. If there is any doubt about a contract, check with an attorney.

2. Keep original contracts in the safety-deposit box. Photocopy contracts for the files.

3. Renewals of contracts, savings certificates, permits, safety-deposit box, etc., must be checked on regularly.

4. The executive board must approve the signing of new contracts and renewals.

Chapter XIII

Office Organization and Management

What records to keep, where to keep them, and for how long soon becomes a problem for even a small organization. All too often the files, consisting of several cardboard cartons filled with unsorted papers, are transferred from one president to another. Important documents such as charters can be lost, insurance policies and contracts cancelled, and reports that would enable chairpersons to function more efficiently are ignored, because the files are not properly organized or are not in the possession of the right person.

The organization's needs and activities will indicate what office space is necessary and what records will be kept. For example, an organization whose aim is to improve nursing-home care may employ a paid ombudsman as a professional executive and use volunteers as nursing-home visitors. Such an organization will require office space, telephone service, files, desks, and typewriters. A small group meeting in restaurants or homes of members may divide its records among the proper officers and chairpersons or may have rented office space that is used only a few hours a week. A large national organization with thousands of members will need office employees and space adequate to handle its business.

Office Requirements: Organizations such as country clubs, condominium owners' associations, nationwide groups with a headquarters building, etc., may hire a professional staff executive, a club manager, or an office manager to run the organization under the direction of the elected officers and the executive board. The paid staff member has the responsibility of carrying out duties delegated by the elected officers.

1. A time-card system for employees must be developed.

2. Records must be kept for salary, social security, and withholding-tax deductions.

3. An office directory of people on call for emergencies, repairs, maintenance, and service is necessary.

4. State and local health and sanitation regulations must be posted.

5. A billing system for members must be established. This includes monthly dues, late charges, extra charges such as greens fees, swim team, lessons, equipment, meals, and guest fees. Executive board policy will determine the procedure regarding delinquent members.

6. The manager should order supplies, subject to the approval of the executive board.

7. The petty cash fund should be reconciled by the auditor at stated intervals.

8. A telephone dial lock should be used to prevent unauthorized telephone use. If possible, long-distance business should be handled by mail. Telephone memos should be routed to the proper person.

9. The office secretary or executive should open all mail addressed to the organization. Mail addressed to individual officers or members should be sent to them, unless prior authority to open it has been given. Mail addressed to a former president must be sent to that officer. Large organizations should develop routine response letters for appeals for donations and questions asked frequently by members. Correspondence must be handled promptly. A reply to a letter should never be scribbled on the bottom of the original letter and returned to the person who wrote it. The organization has no record of the correspondence, and the writer of the original letter is apt to be deeply offended at such a cursory response.

10. A directory with the location of equipment such as fuse boxes, water shut-off valves, etc., should be maintained in the office.

FILING AND STORAGE

The paper work of an organization should be kept to the minimum required to carry out its aims and activities. However, adequate and accessible records are necessary to the continuity of the group and, in the case of a nonprofit, tax-exempt corporation or association, are required by law.

After an organization has been in existence a few years, filing and storage of records become a problem, especially if the group does not have a headquarters or office space. The first step to keeping the records to a manageable size is to be certain that they are placed in the proper file. The following methods of filing will work well for most organizations.

Ready-Reference File: The work of any organization can be more easily accomplished if important papers are kept together in a ready-reference file that is brought to each meeting by the recording secretary. This file should contain:

1. Photocopy of articles of incorporation, charter, or articles of association, or organizing instrument.
2. Bylaws, rules of order, standing rules.
3. Current motions.
4. Budget for year.
5. Photocopies of contracts and insurance policies.
6. Renewal dates of all contracts and permits.

Corporate Record Book: The president of a nonprofit corporation should be in possession of a corporate record book containing the following:

1. Photocopy of articles of incorporation or charter.
2. Bylaws.
3. Tax-exemption letters—state and federal.

4. Copies of minutes.
5. Membership ledger.

Reports: If good and brief reports are made by officers and committee heads at the end of each administration and turned over to their successors, the records can be kept to a manageable size. With a good report, there is no need to keep a volume of correspondence dealing with such things as the year's programs. Copies of reports go to the president and recording secretary.

Safety-Deposit Box: Organizations owning property need a safety-deposit box. The presence of two members, the president and vice-president or treasurer, should be required for access to the box. In it are kept:

1. Articles of incorporation or charter.
2. Bonds and securities.
3. Deeds.
4. Contracts and mortgages.
5. Copyrights.
6. Insurance policies.
7. Inventory of club property, including snapshots, which should be updated each year.

President's File:

1. Corporate record book, if applicable.
2. Yearly reports of officers and committee chairpersons.
3. Important correspondence, with carbons of answers. Be sure to staple incoming envelope with letter.
4. Current membership file.
5. Current budget and monthly financial statements.

Recording Secretary's File:

1. Ready-reference file.
2. Minutes book with bylaws, rules of order, standing rules, and current motions in front, if a ready-reference file is not kept.

3. Copies of officers' and committee chairpersons' reports.
4. Current budget.
5. Copies of contracts, renewal dates, and insurance information.

Treasurer's File:

1. Ledgers and checkbooks.
2. Canceled checks and bank statements.
3. Audit reports.
4. Budgets.
5. Income-tax returns for the past three years. Be sure to check the current Internal Revenue Service ruling.
6. Donations book, if applicable.
7. Membership file, active and dropped members.
8. Paid bills for equipment under warranty and any valuable items such as furniture that might be needed for insurance purposes.

Sorting and Discarding:

1. Segregate important material from unimportant items, which will be kept only for a short period of time. Do not let the unimportant material get into the files.
2. Keep all extraneous material, such as advertisements, out of the files.
3. Discard unnecessary duplicate copies.
4. Keep summaries of statistical records and discard working papers.

How Long to Keep:

1. Check the treasury department regulations regarding all material used in connection with government reports and income tax.
2. If the papers are involved in the defense or prosecution of law suits, check with an attorney before discarding.
3. Consider whether the records are of historical value. Many times files that cannot be duplicated are destroyed.

Where to Keep Storage Files:

1. There may be space in a member's home, but many times this is inadvisable because the material is too bulky or because the officers will not have easy access to the material.

2. In many parts of the country, mini storage space is available at storage companies. Organizations should consider renting this.

3. Microfilming records for storage is recommended for large or long-established organizations. It is not expensive and saves much space. A court of law will accept microfilmed records.

Chapter XIV

Public Relations

Good public relations are essential to the growth of an organization and for the success of programs developed to carry out its purposes. The community will be more supportive of fund-raisers held by the group if its goals and activities are known. People are more likely to make donations to, or become members of, an organization that has built a reputation for worthwhile objectives, special projects that enhance community life, brief business meetings followed by stimulating programs, and enthusiastic, friendly members.

It is essential that members recognize that effective public relations are on-going, and consist of internal and external programs that involve all of them.

INTERNAL PUBLIC RELATIONS

Friendliness: Guests and prospective members must be welcomed at meetings. They must not be left to sit in a corner by themselves or ignored at luncheon or dinner meetings or refreshment periods. All too often the membership chairperson gets prospective members to meetings, only to have them refuse to join because they feel unwelcome. A reputation for unfriendliness can spread throughout the community, with the result that the organization may find it difficult to get support for its programs.

Keeping Members Informed: Internal communication is the lifeline of an organization. If members constantly complain that they don't know what is going on, there is a breakdown in internal communication that needs immediate correction. A membership directory and a calendar of events should be distributed to all members yearly and presented to new members when they join. A monthly or quarterly newsletter will keep members up to date about current activities. A telephone committee should be used to notify members of special meetings and remind them about regular meetings. (See "Duties of Committee Chairpersons," Chapter VI.)

THE NEWSLETTER

The newsletter editor is in charge of writing, editing, and distributing the newsletter, monthly or quarterly, as directed by the executive board.

Contents: Each newsletter should contain:

1. Brief message from the president.
2. Notice of date, place, time, and program for next meeting.
3. Names, addresses, and telephone numbers of new members.
4. Announcements of coming activities, fund-raisers, exhibits, contests, and new developments of interest to members.
5. Brief reports on special events such as conferences, seminars, exhibits, etc.
6. Information on any pending or recently passed legislation pertaining to group's purpose or activities.
7. Report on important decisions made by the executive board.
8. Honors to, or outstanding achievements of, members.

Format: The newsletter must be clear, concise, attractive, and easy-to-read. Reduced type must not be used if most of the members are middle-aged or older. It is better to edit or condense announcements than to crowd too many on a page.

Preparation of the Newsletter:

1. Estimates of printing cost should be obtained from several printers. Consider mimeographing or photocopying to keep down cost.

2. Estimate mailing cost.

3. Get authority from executive board, budget committee, or membership for expense.

4. Make sure certain members are informed of deadlines for mailing information. It is best not to take any items over the telephone.

5. Edit, check spelling of all names, and lay out material.

6. Type camera-ready copy or prepare stencil.

7. Take copy to printer. Try to allow the printer a day or two extra.

Distribution:

1. Mail to all members and to any interested persons that the executive board places on the mailing list.

2. If the newsletter is distributed at meetings, the editor must see that absent members receive a copy.

EXTERNAL PUBLIC RELATIONS

Word-of-Mouth Promotion: All members should consider themselves public relations agents of the organization. Enthusiastic word-of-mouth support is vital for promotion of fund-raising activities.

Speeches Made by Officers: A new organization with a charitable or educational purpose can soon become known in the community, if the president and members of the executive board publicize its activities by making appearances before other groups. Program chairpersons are always looking for speakers and most will welcome the person who desires to make a brief, informative presentation.

Use of the Media: Wise use of newspapers, radio, and television must be directed by the public relations chairperson.

Brochures: An attractive and easy-to-read brochure explaining the organization's purposes and activities should be available at all meetings and special functions. The group's logo should be featured on the brochure.

A logo is a stylized symbol that represents the organization's name or purpose. Examples of well-known logos are the S in a circle used by Safeway Corporation, the shooting star used by Lockheed, and the caduceus that represents the medical profession. A conservation group might choose a simplified depiction of an oak or redwood tree. A writer's organization could select a quill pen. The logo should be original, distinctive, and easy to reproduce. It should be used not only on brochures, but also on stationery, flyers, posters, and any other printed material put out by the organization.

Essentials of a Good Brochure:

1. It must be attractive and eye-catching.
2. It must be easy to read.
3. It should feature the organization's logo.
4. It should contain a description of the organization's purposes and activities.
5. It should list the officers and directors or executive board.
6. It should be brief.
7. It should be inexpensive to reproduce. It is a mistake for a nonprofit organization to spend a great deal of money on graphics or heavy paper.
8. It should be designed so that it can be reproduced on standard or legal-sized paper and folded for mailing.
9. It should be made available to the people whose support the organization desires to attract. Brochures kept in storage do no good.

How to Write a Good Brochure:

1. Explain what the group is. Example:

WHAT ARE FRIENDS OF THE PUBLIC LIBRARY?

A well-known children's book is titled, *A Friend is Someone Who Likes You*. The Maintown Public Library has its Friends, both official and unknown. This is to tell you what Friends are, and do, and to invite your support. Friends groups are a traditional part of a library's program and are organized by interested citizens who want to assist the library in achieving its goals. In some states, the Friends are organized in a special section of the State Library Association. The Maintown Friends of the Library was organized in early 1978 and was incorporated in the spring of 1979.

2. List the purposes. Example:

—to maintain an association of people interested in books and libraries.
—to supplement the library's total program by participating in volunteer activities and encouraging donations of books, endowments, and bequests.
—to focus public attention on library services, facilities, and needs.

3. Briefly explain some of the activities included. Example:

—providing the library with a regular volunteer group that performs routine tasks, freeing the staff for other duties.
—raising funds to purchase special materials and equipment not provided for in the regular budget, through book sales and a variety of special events.
—assisting the library with such activities as the annual New Teachers' Tea, Children's Book Week, and National Library Week.
—providing a series of programs and study groups on books, reading, and related topics for members.

—working with and through professional and community associations to inform others about the library.
—sponsoring the Junior Friends, a group of children interested in helping the library and participating in special programs.
—seeking out and stimulating gifts of local historical material such as letters, diaries, and other ephemera for preservation in the library.

4. Give information on membership and dues. Example:

Friends of the Maintown Public Library welcome to membership all those who are interested in the library. The ultimate responsibility for the quality of library service rests with the citizens. Membership in the Friends is a means of showing your interest and support. Won't you join today?

> Regular annual membership ..... $ 1.00
> Junior members, under 18 .... .50
> Contributing members 5.00
> Sustaining members 10.00
> Patrons 25.00

Organizations are invited to join as patrons. Members are encouraged to serve on various committees, but inactive Friends are welcome.

5. List the names, addresses, and telephone numbers (optional) of the officers and directors. Include the membership chairperson.
6. A library, museum, opera, or symphony support group might include a brief history of the institution. Example:

SOME FACTS ABOUT YOUR LIBRARY

The Maintown Public Library was established as a city library in November 1960. Prior to that it had been a branch of the Mountain County Free Library System. The present building was designed by John Jones, A.I.A. The library is nearly 60,000 square feet and has a book capacity of 300,000 volumes. Circulation for 1979 was 1,500,000 volumes. The library serves the City of Maintown and is supported solely by revenues and taxes paid to the city. It is administered by the city librarian, assisted by an advisory board of library trustees appointed by the city council for four-year terms.

Library hours are:

> Monday through Friday 9:00 A.M. to 9:00 P.M.
> Saturday . . . . 9:00 A.M. to 6:00 P.M.
> Sunday . . . . 1:00 P.M. to 5:00 P.M.

7. A membership application may be included as a part of the brochure. Sample:

Mail with check to Jane Jones,   Enclosed is _____dues.
100 Union St.   (Name)   _____(Tel.)   _____
Maintown, TX 00000   (Address)   _____

8. The layout and printing of the brochure is also important. The paper should be folded in thirds and the material laid out in columns, so that the organization's name and logo appear on the front. Both sides of the paper are used. It is best to put the membership application on the reverse of the third that contains the name and logo. The applicant may want to keep the information in the rest of the brochure. Three bids, in writing, should be obtained for the printing. Nonprofit, tax-exempt organizations often solicit contributions from local banks and business firms to defray printing costs. Acknowledgement of this is made in the brochure.

DUTIES OF THE PUBLIC RELATIONS CHAIRPERSON

Upon accepting the appointment, the chairperson should confer with the president, the program chairperson, and anyone in the group who has helpful connections with the media to plan publicity for the coming year. All publicity regarding the organization should be released by the public relations chairperson. This policy should be established by the executive board and clearly understood by all the members.

USE OF THE MEDIA

Preliminary Procedure:

1. Visit editors of local papers and discuss with them the purposes of your group. It is best to make an appointment with the managing editor, the sports editor, or the editor of the community living or activities pages, depending on the activities of your group. Avoid telephoning or calling upon an editor during the hours before the paper's deadlines.

2. Ask for the newspaper's policies regarding organizations like yours and their deadlines for releases.

3. Find out if they will take a follow-up story and how they prefer that you arrange for pictures.

4. Investigate educational radio and television stations for the possibility of interviews with the organization's officers about the group's purposes and projects.

5. Remember that metropolitan papers will print news of interest to a large segment of readers. Small town papers use news about leading individuals in the community, outstanding events, and notices of meetings.

6. Investigate the use of calendars of events sponsored by banks and business firms.

7. Consider advertising and get the rates.

8. Remember that columnists may be glad to get unusual items about your group. Mention in a column can attract more attention than a short news story.

Learn and Comply With Newspaper Usage:

1. Type and double space all copy.

2. Put your name and title, telephone number, and the name of the organization in the upper left hand corner.

3. Put the release date (the date you prefer to have the story used) or "for immediate release" in the upper right-hand corner.

4. Be concise and accurate.

5. Be certain all names are spelled correctly.

6. Who, what, when, where, why, and how are essentials of a news release. Put them into the first paragraph—the release may be cut.

7. Remember that names make news.

8. Do not send carbons or photocopies. Editors are apt to ignore stories if they know the identical release is going to five papers in the area.

9. Provide facts, not opinions. Do not exaggerate, editorialize, personalize, or emotionalize. Use a news approach.

10. The editor cannot be asked to write the story. Write it yourself. Do not send brochures or programs in place of a story.

11. Copy goes only to one editor per paper. Select the appropriate editor.

12. Do not tell editors how to use your stories. Keep relations on a cordial and friendly basis.

13. Observe deadlines. Do not dash in at the last minute and expect that your story will be rushed into print.

14. Do not harangue the editor if a release is cut or omitted. Approach the editor in a friendly manner and ask for the reason, so that you may rectify it, if possible. Remember that editors are human, and many organizations compete for limited space.

15. Keep a carbon. Newspapers can make mistakes. You may need your carbon to convince an irate member that you did not misspell a name.

16. Political-action groups may find their releases cut or ignored because of the paper's ownership policy. They should consider letters to the editors, small weekly papers, and paid advertisements.

Photographs:

1. Most newspapers will use photographs, from snapshot-size on up to eight by tens. Check with the editor to see if local papers have a different policy.

2. Photographs must be clear black-and-white glossies with good contrast. Never send polaroids.

3. When a professional photographer—yours or the newspaper's—is used, have everything ready in advance. The people must be there and any props prepared. Give clear directions about date, time, and place, and include a telephone number where you can be reached.

4. If the photographs are being taken by a member of the organization, make certain the paper's requirements are understood. Supply the editor with several selections so that an appropriate choice can be made.

5. Action pictures, showing people doing things, are desired. Avoid a line-up of people. Smiling faces are more pleasing. Identify from left to right.

6. It is best to take outdoor pictures early in the morning or late in the afternoon. Avoid harsh noonday sun.

7. Supply a self-addressed, stamped envelope if you want photographs returned.

8. Photographs furnished by speakers or entertainers should be returned to them.

Regular and Program Meetings: Get information from the president and program chairperson about the meeting and program or speaker at least three weeks in advance. This includes a biography and picture of the speaker. Try to put something about the organization's purposes and activities in each release.

SAMPLE RELEASE

SAVE OCEANCITY, INC. *For immediate release*

Jane Smith, Public Relations Chairperson
426-4795

The Save Oceancity organization will hold a regular meeting and program September 14 at 1P.M. at the Midtown Community Center, 1100 Main Street.

John Jones, chairperson of the South Carolina Coastal Commission, will speak on "The Dangers to our Shores." Jones, who was appointed last week to the United States Oceanology Commission, has an article, "Our Ocean: Fair or Foul," in the August issue of *Two Continents* magazine. A question-and-answer period will follow the speech.

According to Mary Smith, President of Save Oceancity, Inc., the group was founded to oppose the 440-unit housing development planned for White Ranch. The public is invited to attend the meeting.

PUBLICITY FOR FUND-RAISERS AND OTHER SPECIAL EVENTS

Plan the Campaign:

1. The publicity chairperson should confer with the general chairperson of the event four to six months in advance, to decide what kinds of publicity are needed.

2. Consider newspaper stories, community calendar announcements, paid advertising, flyers, posters, direct mail, and television and radio public service announcements.

3. The chairperson needs a committee when many avenues of publicity are being used. The committee assists with the design and distribution of posters and flyers, addressing envelopes for mailings, and stapling multipage programs.

Obtain All Necessary Information: Get the purpose, event, date, time, place, price, speakers, entertainers, pictures and biographies, name and address of person in charge of reservations, and cut-off date for reservations.

Prepare a Newspaper Release: Include the date of release, name of organization, type of event, purpose, date, time, place, speaker, entertainers, or artists, name of president, name of general chairperson, and ticket information. It is nice to send a complimentary ticket to the editor and to follow up with a thank you note.

SAMPLE RELEASE

SAVE OCEANCITY, INC. *For immediate release*

Jane Smith, Public Relations Chairperson
426-4795

The Save Oceancity organization will stage a wine-tasting fund-raiser September 14, from 6 to 9 P.M., at South Gallery, 100 Main Street.

According to Chairpersons Mary Paget and Betty Moore, funds will be used to oppose the 440-unit housing development planned for the White Ranch. President Mary Smith announces that John Jones, chairperson of the South Carolina Coastal Commission, will be present to answer questions.

Tickets may be purchased at the gallery or by calling Judy Long, 438-0000 or Tom Gray, 000-1111.

T-shirts with the Save Oceancity insignia will be for sale, and wines, cheese and crackers will be featured, along with music by the Great Days Music Company of Greendale and folk singer Marie Danes.

Flyers: These can be distributed, with permission, in libraries, museums, other public buildings, at meetings of related organizations, passed out on the street (check with the police department as to whether a permit is necessary), or mailed. Be sure all essential information is on the flyer, including directions if the location is hard to find.

Mailing List can be obtained from members who submit names of friends, from the guest book, by borrowing the mailing list of other organizations, and by keeping a record of people who have attended past events.

SAMPLE FLYER

STOP THE HOUSES   SAVE THE RANCH
SAVE OCEANCITY

Join Us at a Wine-tasting Party,
September 14, 6-9 P.M.
at
SOUTH GALLERY, 1100 MAIN STREET

Wine • Cheese • Crackers
Music By
GREAT DAYS MUSIC COMPANY
FOLK SINGER MARIE DANES

Donation $5.00
SPONSORED BY SAVE OCEANCITY, INC.

Mail with check to Mary Paget 111 Rose Ave. Oceancity, SC 11111 by Sept. 7.	Please reserve _____ tickets at $5.00 ea. for the Save Oceancity Wine-tasting Name _____ Address _____

Posters should be attractive and eye-catching. Large, easy-to-read letters are a must. They are placed in stores, churches, libraries, lobbies of public buildings, banks, and on utility poles. Permission to display the poster must be obtained. In some cities, ordinances prohibit posting bills on utility poles. Be sure to check first. Give your organization a favorable image by removing the posters the day after the event.

Radio and Television Announcements giving all essential information are written by the public relations chairperson. Time allowed may be ten or sixty seconds.

SAMPLE RELEASE

The Friends of the Bigtown Public Library will hold a giant used-book sale Saturday, August 19th, from 9 A.M. to 5 P.M., in the library parking lot, 7th and Main Streets. Proceeds from the sale will be used to buy a microfilm reader for the library.

Membership Participation: All members should assist in the publicity for a large event by making announcements to organizations to which they belong, by word-of-mouth publicity, and by telephoning their friends.

Program: The design, layout, and printing of a program for the event may be part of the public relations chairperson's duties. In some organizations this task is given to a program committee appointed for that purpose. An attractive cover enhances a program. The logo, a short history of the organization, its purposes, the names of the president, general chairperson, all committee chairpersons, and committee members are included. Special acknowledgement is made of all merchants and firms that have assisted with the event.

Printing: If a member has access to a mimeograph machine, flyers, posters, and programs can be reproduced inexpensively with the group paying only the cost of materials. Bids from three printers must be obtained if the work is done by a commercial firm. In some localities it is best to use a union shop.

PUBLICITY FOR CONVENTIONS AND OTHER SPECIAL EVENTS

Good publicity is essential for special events, such as one-day conferences, workshops, seminars, art fairs, etc., that are sponsored as cultural or educational contributions to community life. Information about these events must be distributed as widely as possible, so that the public will attend. On the other hand, the success of a state or national convention depends upon getting information about the programs and events planned to the organization's members. The material should be presented in complete and exciting stories that will stimulate registration. A convention, however, may be newsworthy in itself, either because of action taken or resolutions passed by the organization, or because the speakers and/or entertainers are nationally known. Duties of the public relations chairperson follow those outlined previously in this chapter. The following procedures will help the chairperson to obtain additional publicity.

Series of Releases: For a one-day or weekend conference, a release containing all details, including the speakers' names, can be sent to the paper a month in advance. This can be followed with weekly stories, giving the background and qualifications in detail of one or two speakers. Glossy photographs should be included. A series of releases such as this should be discussed with the editor.

Interviews: Arrangements may be made for well-known speakers, entertainers, and national officers to appear on television or radio or be interviewed by a reporter. Permission must be obtained from the persons to be interviewed. The editor or television or radio producer should be approached well in advance of the event. The persons responsible for educational and local television programs are more likely to be responsive than those producing major network shows. Transportation to the studio should be provided interviewees.

Coverage of the Event: Local newspapers can be invited to send reporters to conferences or seminars. The invitation should consist of a letter to the editor, inviting the paper to send a reporter. The purpose of the event, a program, the organization's brochure, and background material on the speakers should be included. If a fee is charged, an admission and meal ticket are enclosed. If the speech is made from a head table following a meal, arrangements should be made for the reporter to sit at a table directly in front of the speaker. Advance copies of speeches should be supplied, if possible.

Press Room: If members of the press are invited to cover a state or national convention, a room should be made available for their use. The location should be close to the banquet and meeting rooms. Typewriters, paper, desks, chairs, and telephones should be provided. Hot coffee is a nice touch.

Press Table: A table should be reserved for the press, directly in front of the head table, when speeches are made at a luncheon or banquet. Meal tickets are furnished by the organization.

Background Information about the organization, issues to be covered, national officers, candidates (if elections will be held), speakers, and entertainers should be given out to all reporters. Convention programs must be available.

Press Conference: If developments or announcements are important enough, or when election results are known, a press conference may be called. All reporters covering the event should be alerted in ample time to attend. The room chosen should be large enough so that it is not crowded. Adequate seating, lighting, and ventilation are essential. The public relations chairperson should introduce the person who will make the presentation. Typed advance copies of the material should be distributed. The presence of members of the executive board or other members of the organization who can add to the presentation, give background material, or answer questions is desirable.

Liaison With the Press: The public relations chairperson, or a member of the committee, should be available at all times, to answer reporters' questions and offer assistance. All news regarding the convention should be released by, or with prior approval of, the public relations chairperson. Releases may be distributed by various committee heads and officers, but they must first be cleared through the chairperson. This procedure prevents duplication and allows the chairperson to coordinate press coverage.

Newspaper Clippings: Following any meeting, conference, special event, or convention, the public relations chairperson sends newspaper clippings to all those who appeared on the program.

Chapter XV

Fund Raising

While the members' yearly dues cover actual running expenses, most organizations rely on fund raising to finance the activities that are their reason for existing. These goals can include community improvement, cultural and educational enrichment, charitable donations, support of sports programs, and delegates' expenses for lobbying purposes.

Your parents' club may want to raise $8,000 to send your high school's award-winning band to march in the next inauguration parade. Maybe your "Preserve Clean Air" organization wants to send two members to Washington, D.C. to lobby against the projected easing of smokestack regulations. Perhaps your garden club wishes to beautify the banks of a river bisecting your city. The members are willing to dig, fertilize, and plant, but there's no money available for seed and shrubs. Your art association's bylaws call for a yearly award of two $100 scholarships, and there's only $100 in the treasury. Fund raising is necessary if the group is to meet its goal.

The Plus Side of Fund Raising: Raising money is not always just hard work. It can be fun, and many times some glory rubs off on the organization. Your group will become better known if it makes a civic, cultural, educational, or volunteer contribution and will be considered a community asset. Friendships will develop among

145

members who work together. Using their time and energy for a worthwhile purpose will give them a feeling of pride and accomplishment. The fund-raiser itself may fulfill a community need by providing an afternoon of fun at a carnival, an informative speaker, an opportunity to buy a baked-from-scratch cake, or by giving craftspersons a place to sell their products.

Fund-Raising Pitfalls and How to Overcome Them:

1. *Lack of planning.* The general chairperson plans the affair in detail, with the help of committee members. The president and executive board are kept informed of the committee's progress through regular reports.

2. *Conflicting dates.* Set the date as far ahead as possible and publicize it. Your group could suggest that a community calendar be kept, as a community service, by the chamber of commerce or other central organization.

3. *Repeating the same old thing.* While your members may bake the best cakes in the county, they may want to get out of the kitchen. Even if your organization's carnival, rummage sale, or food booth has a terrific reputation and makes a huge profit, don't make the mistake of repeating it year after year without enthusiastic support from the membership. Variety can add willing workers and spice to fund raising.

4. *Always depending on the same people.* Don't call on the same people to serve as committee heads or workers year in, year out. Jane Tooms may be great at handling reservations, but after five years of it, she might like a chance to make decorations, be a hostess, or take a rest. New members should be given a chance to demonstrate their ability.

5. *Acts of God.* Pick your date to avoid bad weather. If the general chairperson suddenly becomes ill, the cochairperson should be able to take charge. If a fire destroys the selected restaurant the week before a sold-out dinner, it may be possible to move the event to another place, or it might have to be cancelled and the ticket money refunded.

6. *Failure to cover costs.* "It was a great success, but we didn't

make any money" are disheartening words. Usually the cause is poor budgeting and failure to estimate expenses properly. Expenses should be held down if at all possible. If the fund raiser actually loses money, the deficit should be paid from the treasury. Members should not be asked for contributions, and no one member should make up a deficit.

Choice of Project: Keeping in mind the number and abilities of the members and the amount of money needed, the president and the executive board should present to the general membership a choice of fund-raising projects. Wholehearted and enthusiastic support of everyone is essential, therefore the aims and interests of the members must be considered. A symphony auxiliary would push tickets to a musical evening under the stars, featuring champagne and selection from light opera, but might balk if the entertainment was to be provided by a hard-rock group.

The parents' club might find it impossible to raise the money by holding car washes and bake sales, but a large and well-advertised rummage sale could bring in $8,000. So might tying the project to a local event that attracts huge numbers of people from out of the area. An organization operated a food booth at the Antique Airplane Fly-in at the Watsonville, California, airport in June, 1979, and cleared over $8,000 by selling French-fried artichokes, a local delicacy.

Selecting the Date: Once the actual project is chosen, selection of the right date is vitally important. For a large affair, a rummage sale to be held in a municipal auditorium, or a dinner with a well-known speaker with a projected sale of 500 tickets, or a luncheon fashion show at a popular restaurant, it can be necessary to make a reservation a year in advance in order to get the desired accommodations.

Times to avoid are March to mid-April for the obvious tax reasons and the two weeks before Christmas, when most people are extremely busy. Thanksgiving, Memorial Day, Fourth of July, and Labor Day weekends, and the high school and college graduation dates in June are also poor dates for fund-raisers.

Late spring, summer, and early fall are best for out-of-doors events. January and February should be avoided in the northern part of the country because of danger of snow, ice, and flu epidemics. Most groups finds that September (after the start of school) and October are good months for money-raising events.

Try to avoid a conflict of dates with another organization, especially one planning the same type of affair. Since many groups hold annual fund-raisers, it can be wise to check the newspapers of the previous year to see what was scheduled.

Announce the date and project as early as possible. This will alert other organizations to the potential conflict, and they will be able to plan accordingly.

Appointment of the Chairperson and Cochairperson: The member responsible for planning and running the function should be appointed by the president early in the administration. The chairperson, especially for a large fund-raiser, must be dependable, be able to work with the members, have the ability to plan in detail and to delegate authority, and have the flexibility to take in stride and handle last minute minor disasters. She/he must be enthusiastic about the project and willing to accept the job. It is a grave mistake to talk a member into reluctantly taking on the responsibility for this kind of project.

The cochairperson should be a member with the ability to take over at the last minute if necessary and someone who can work in harmony with the chairperson.

Choosing the Place: This depends on the project—a restaurant, if a luncheon or dinner is scheduled; an auditorium or vacant store, for a large rummage sale; the home of a member with a spacious yard, for a tag sale of household and craft items donated by members; or sidewalk space in a busy shopping center, for a bake sale. Sometimes community centers can be rented by nonprofit groups. Fraternal and social halls are available in many localities. The president and the chairperson should tour the available facilities and make a recommendation to the executive board or general membership for approval. Be sure to check the number of people allowed in the room or building according to fire regulations, safety exits, smoking rules, lighting, and restrooms. Parking facilities should be adjacent and well lighted if the affair is to be held at night.

The Contract: Once the place is decided upon, it is imperative that a contract be signed with the owner or manager. Do not depend upon verbal assurance that the facility will be available a year later, not even if you see your group's name written into the reservation book. (See "Contracts, Insurance, and Permits," Chapter XII.)

Duties of the General Chairperson: These will vary with the fund-raiser, but generally the following duties apply to all chairpersons. If the general chairperson sets up a loose-leaf notebook, with sections for budget, copies of correspondence, duties of committee heads, names and telephone numbers of committee members, and their responsibilities, equipment needed, etc. she/he will have a ready reference file which will be especially helpful the day of the event.

The cochairperson should be frequently consulted and must be kept up-to-date on all planning and decisions. If desired, meetings with committee heads can be handled by the cochairperson.

A TIMETABLE FOR FUND RAISERS

One Year Ahead: Select date and reserve place.

Six Months Ahead:

1. Check with city hall, to see if a permit is required to hold a fund-raiser. Some cities, such as Los Angeles, have strict regulations regarding the expense of fund raising. You may have to secure a permit before the event and file a report afterwards.

2. The general chairperson should work out a budget, estimating all anticipated expenses such as publicity, equipment, entertainment, and decoration costs. This can be done with the help of the committee heads. The fee charged should be set to allow for a reasonable profit after expenses are met.

If the event requires an advance ticket sale or a guaranteed attendance, a break-even point must be determined and a deadline set for the sale of the necessary tickets. The organization must be prepared to cancel the affair or pick up a loss, if expenses are not covered.

3. Appoint the committee heads. (In the case of a large rummage sale or book sale, these appointments are made a year in advance.) In some organizations the appointments are made by the president; others give the general chairperson this responsibility. Committees can be needed for setup, cleanup, ticket sales, decorations, favors, door prizes, signs, public relations, lighting, equipment, and ticket-takers or cashiers. The general chairperson meets with all of the committee heads to outline their duties and go over their budgets.

4. Speakers or entertainers. (See "Duties of Other Officers," Chapter V).

Three Months Ahead: Arrangements should be made for any printing that will be needed. Direction signs and posters for use in store windows can be made by members with artistic ability.

Two Months Ahead:

1. If the organization is part of a state or nationwide association, inform all chapters or branches within easy driving distance about your fund-raiser and invite them to attend or buy tickets.

2. Check with state and local tax authorities about sales-tax regulations. In some localities, a resale license is required to sell donated material. A permit from the city may be necessary to hold a garage or tag sale.

3. Look into state and local health regulations regarding the sale of food, used bedding, mattresses, and overstuffed furniture.

4. If you are advertising that contributions to your event are tax-deductible, make certain that your organization has a tax-exemption letter from the Internal Revenue Service.

One Month Ahead:

1. Check with the public relations chairperson to see that publicity is started. (See "Public Relations," Chapter XIV.)

2. Hold a committee meeting. Try to anticipate any problems, and check every detail of planning with the committee heads.

3. See that flyers are distributed and posters put into store windows.

4. Investigate the need for insurance. It may be wise to take out a one-day liability policy for the event. Make arrangements with an insurance agent.

5. Prepare a timetable for the project, and distribute it to all working members. This should include the exact time each committee member should arrive and any special instructions.

Two Weeks Ahead: Reconfirm arrangements with speaker or entertainers.

One Week Ahead:

1. Recheck facility and arrangements with owner or manager.

2. Talk with all committee heads to be certain they are carrying out their duties. Make sure all necessary help will be available. Remind them to notify you immediately if an emergency prevents them from carrying out their duties.

The Day:

1. Stay as flexible and relaxed as possible. Things will go wrong, but probably you'll be the only one who will know it.

2. Carry your notebook with you. Don't trust your memory.

3. Check all equipment ahead of time.

4. Make arrangements with your cochairperson so that one of you will be available at all times.

Afterwards:

1. Count the money with the cashiers, and check the receipt books or ticket records. Turn the money over to the treasurer, along with a full financial report, which includes expenses. In some groups, all money is sent to the treasurer by the ticket chairperson as it is

received, and all bills are paid from the treasury. In others, the general chairperson is given a fund to cover estimated expenses.

2. Send thank you letters to speaker, entertainers, and to manager of facility. Thank all committee heads and members. Give them full credit for a wonderful job.

3. Make out a complete report for the president, with a copy to the recording secretary. Keep a copy for your file.

4. Turn your notebook and report over to the next chairperson, for use as a planning guide, if the affair is to be an annual event.

A USED-BOOK SALE

Many literary groups and groups that support public libraries find this an effective fund-raiser. About a year is needed to collect enough donations to hold a successful sale. Your group may be able to put a bin in the lobby of the library, where patrons can deposit books. The main problem is storage of books and finding a place to price them. Sometimes space is available in the basement of the library or in an unused portion of a city or county-owned building.

If the proceeds of the sale are used to benefit the library, it may be possible to hold the sale on the library parking lot or grounds. Because the setup is time-consuming, it is best to do this the day before. One Friends group asks a Boy Scout troop, as a part of their community service work, to sleep on the grounds overnight to guard the books.

Committees Needed: General chairperson, sorting and pricing, setup, book-selling, food and drink, information and courtesy, cleanup.

Duties of the Sorting and Pricing Committee: The chairperson should be a member who is knowledgeable about the values of old books. A large number of workers is needed, so that no one member has to put in too many hours. The committee works throughout the year, sorting the books into categories, such as mysteries, juveniles, science fiction, fiction, nonfiction, and texts, and packing them into labeled boxes. The committee is free to discard soiled or badly damaged books.

Most books are priced at 25¢ for hardbacks and 10¢ for paperbacks. Valuable books may be found in the thousands of donations. These should be set aside and priced accordingly. The pricers should check to see if the book is autographed, a numbered copy, a sought-after first edition, or a rare out-of-print book. Books that are apt to have added value are those on Americana, railroading, early airplanes and automobiles, World War I and II, and first editions of such authors as Hemingway, Faulkner, Frost, Maugham, and Wolfe. Many books published in the twenties and thirties by such writers as Ethel M. Dell and Gene Stratton Porter are now hunted by collectors. Books illustrated by Frank Godwin, Louis Agassiz Fuertes, Maxfield Parrish, and N.C. Wyeth are also in demand.

Members of the pricing committee need to develop a feel for the unusual or rare book. They should check them with *Gold in Your Attic* by Van Allen Bradley, *5,000 Old Books With Up-To-Date Prices* published by Schroeders, Route 4, Paducah, Kentucky 42001, or *American Book Prices Current,* a reference book available in most libraries. The pricers can also get an idea of what is currently wanted by going through several copies of the *AB Bookman's Weekly* and by touring used-book stores. A treasure or rare-books table is set aside for the valuable books.

It will not be possible to sort out all of the books with added value. The committee should not feel chagrined if a $20 book is sold for a quarter. These sales are popular with the public because of the possibility of finding a rare book at a bargain price. Because book dealers frequently descend on book sales *en masse* at the opening hour, some organizations limit the sale to members for the first hour. Admission is by membership card. Publicizing this membership benefit increases interest in the group and may make a separate membership drive unnecessary.

Committees that do not want to go through the work of screening and pricing books sell them for 25¢ an inch. Since the average hardback is an inch wide, this works out to about the same price. The disadvantage is that rare and collectible books go for a quarter.

Duties of the Setup Committee: The hard work for this committee comes either the night before or early on the day of the sale. The physical layout is planned ahead and drawn out on paper. Sufficient tables to display the books are either rented or borrowed. It may be possible to use the library's tables.

Signs are needed for designation of special categories of books. They can be cardboard signs mounted on wooden sticks and placed in coffee cans filled with sand. The grounds should be roped off and a checkout table placed at the front of the area. The committee will have to unpack and arrange the books on the tables. Extra books can be left in boxes.

Duties of the Book-Selling Committee: It is a good idea to have four cashiers for the first two hours to avoid long lines of customers. After that, two cashiers at a time are sufficient. They will need cashboxes, paper bags, ample change, and adding machines, receipt books, or paper to total prices. Other workers straighten book tables as the sale progresses and set out books left in boxes. A couple of members should be assigned to patrol the perimeters of the grounds so that boxes of books are not carried off without payment.

The Food and Drink Committee: Many organizations find that selling lemonade and hot dogs or cookies is an added moneymaker. A booth is needed for this. Waste containers are placed nearby. Check to see if a permit is required.

Information and Courtesy Center: Information about your organization's activities and goals can be distributed from a booth that also serves as a lost-and-found and first-aid center. The usual lost items are children who have wandered away from their parents. First aid should not be administered by your volunteer workers. In case of an accident or the collapse of a patron, the fire department paramedics or the appropriate agency must be called. Place the information booth and the cashiers' tables in the shade or provide patio umbrellas. Many times stores that carry outdoor furniture will lend umbrellas.

Cleanup Committee: This committee packs up all leftover books and tidies the grounds. Waste containers must be emptied, and all borrowed equipment returned. Arrangements are made ahead of time for disposal of unsold books or space for storage until the next sale.

FASHION SHOW

Advantages:

1. Popular fund-raiser for women's organizations.

2. Expenses are low, and a minimum amount of work is required.

3. Can be held at a restaurant, around pool setting, in clubhouse of private club, or in garden of a private home.

4. Can be tied to a theme. Try to work in originality by showing some fashions for men or vintage costumes. Styles from the Roaring Twenties, costumes from other countries, or 1890s apparel will add spice.

Disadvantages:

1. Tickets may be hard to sell, because many groups use this method of fund raising.

2. Some restaurants schedule regular fashion shows as a noontime attraction.

3. The restaurant may require a guaranteed attendance.

4. If members or their children are used as models, jealousy can arise on the part of those not chosen.

Committees Needed: General chairperson, tickets, public relations, decorations, door prizes, setup, models, food, program, cleanup.

Place: A fashion show can be held in a restaurant in conjunction with a luncheon. A country club or swim-and-tennis club may decide to hold a fashion show and tea, cocktail, or wine-tasting party around its pool. A fashion show held in a private garden setting may feature such refreshments as the organization wishes—luncheon (catered or prepared by the group), punch and small sandwiches, if late in the afternoon. The facility must have adequate dressing rooms for the models and a space to hang the clothing.

Date: The best dates are early in the fashion season: early spring for spring or summer clothes; early fall for winter fashions.

Arrangements with Store: Medium-sized specialty shops are the best stores to approach for cooperation with a fashion show. The owner, ready-to-wear manager, or fashion buyer knows how to stage a show and can give good advice. One of them may act as the commentator or can recommend someone to do this.

Ticket Chairperson:

1. Arranges for printing of tickets and distributes them to all members.
2. Keeps a record of the number of tickets members have to sell.
3. Checks carefully on how ticket sale is going a couple of weeks before the event.
4. Makes arrangements for tickets to be collected at door of facility or at luncheon table.
5. Collects ticket money from members and gives it to treasurer.

Public Relations Chairperson: (See "Public Relations" Chapter XIV.)

Door Prizes:

1. Check first to see if this is legal in your area.
2. Merchandise and gift certificates can be solicited from merchants in the area.
3. If the purchase of an admission ticket includes the chance of winning a door prize, the ticket is designed so that one half of it can be deposited in a box from which prize winners are drawn.
4. If chances on door prizes are sold separately, rolls of double

tickets are purchased at a stationery store. One half remains in the possession of the guest; the matching half is deposited in a decorated box. Raffle tickets can be priced at three or five for a dollar, to make their sale easier and give those attending an opportunity for fun.

5. The general chairperson or the president draws the winning tickets from the box at an intermission halfway through the show.

Decorations: The decorations chairperson works out a theme, and her committee makes and sets up the decorations. This committee is asked to spend as little as possible. Large centerpieces are a nuisance; small inexpensive decorations can be contrived from such things as plastic tomato boxes filled with bouquets of homegrown flowers. Arrangements of greens can be used.

Equipment: This committee is responsible for arranging the room so that the models can be seen. If the restaurant is spacious and the tables are not crowded together, the models can walk between them. If this is not possible, a ramp and raised runway or platform is necessary. Some restaurants have this equipment, or it can be rented. If the runway is put together by the committee, precautions must be taken so that it is safe and does not wobble. When steps are used at the end of a runway, someone must be stationed there to assist the models off the platform. Additional lighting focused on the runway may be required. The commentator will need a loudspeaker system.

Model Committee: The model committee selects the models with the approval of the general chairperson. The choice is dictated by the fashion coordinator from the store, who will request one or two models each in four or five specific sizes. The store can furnish the models, or the organization may use members, chosen by lot from among those wishing to participate.

The chairperson makes appointments at the store for the models to try on the fashions they will wear. Accessories are planned with each model, if these are not furnished by the store.

Arrangements are made with the facility so that the fashions can be delivered at least an hour before the show. The chairperson checks that the delivery includes all of the clothes. A committee member brings hair spray, Scotch tape, straight pins, tissues, hair pins—anything that the models may need and forget.

Food: If a restaurant is chosen, the general chairperson selects the menu and sees that the items, price, tax, and tip are included in the contract.

The easiest way to serve food in a private club or home is to have it catered. The menu should be selected well in advance, and a contract that includes all items to be furnished and the price should be signed.

If the luncheon is to be prepared by members, committees to cook and serve the food, and to clean up afterward are needed. Many groups have held successful afternoon events by asking members to donate plates of small cookies and dainty sandwiches to set out on a buffet table.

Since serving a member-prepared luncheon in a private club for a hundred or so guests is a difficult task, a salad luncheon is best. Members are asked to donate seafood, potato, macaroni, gelatin, or green salads, fruit, relishes, pickles, rolls and butter, or simple desserts. The food is arranged so that the guests can serve themselves from two sides of a buffet table. Members, acting as waitresses, serve beverages and see that water glasses are filled. They clear the tables and offer dessert before the fashion show begins.

Program: The committee in charge of the program sees that it is printed and distributed to each seat or given out at the door. The program gives a brief history of the organization, its purposes and activities, lists committee heads and members, the president, the general chairperson, the models, the store furnishing the fashions, the commentator, the performers if any, the donors of door prizes, and any special acknowledgements.

Background Music: Either piano, organ, or small combo may be used for background music during the luncheon and show. It must be soft and not drown out the commentator.

Rehearsal: Always necessary. It is arranged for several days in advance with the fashion commentator, whoever is coordinating from the store, general chairperson, model committee, and models. The store owner may not want the actual clothes used, but the models should walk through the routine and the music should be played.

Actual Show: The general chairperson welcomes the guests, thanks the committees, asks the president to say a few words, and introduces the commentator. If there is a head table, the chairperson arranges the seating, sets out place cards, and introduces everyone sitting there. An agenda should be prepared in advance to make certain there are no omissions. The commentator speaks briefly about fashions or the store and then asks the first model to appear.

BAKE SALE

The bake sale is a simple way to raise fifty to two hundred dollars. Once the date and place are decided upon by the president and executive board or by vote of the members, the telephone committee calls all members and asks for donations of baked goods or paper bags and plastic wrap. Before the sale is planned, it is important to check with local authorities for permits and regulations regarding the sale of home-baked goods.

Disadvantages:

1. Too often members resent being asked to both donate and buy baked goods.
2. If an organization has too many bake sales, members may decide it would be cheaper and easier to donate the money and refuse to work on the sale.
3. Donated items made from mixes can alienate buyers.
4. Arrangements must be made to postpone or get indoors in case of bad weather.

5. Sales can be slow, because people are becoming calorie and cholesterol conscious.

Committees Needed: General chairperson, telephone, pickup, sales.

Dates: The Saturday before Easter is a good date for a bake sale. Food bazaars, which are sales of baked goods and items that can be used as gifts, such as home-canned specialties, candies, pickles, and jams, are frequently held early in December.

Place: Many locally owned markets will allow bake sales in front of their stores or in their parking lots. Food bazaars can be held in church halls, rented stores, and at schools. Swim and tennis clubs have been especially successful with bake sales held in their clubhouses on the Saturdays before Easter and Christmas.

Publicity: Members are reminded of the sale through the newsletter. The public relations chairperson sends a release to local papers and puts up posters if necessary.

Duties of General Chairperson:

1. Checks with the telephone chairperson two weeks in advance, to find out how many items have been promised.

2. Makes arrangements to have items picked up that cannot be delivered.

3. Sees that there are adequate tables and wrapping material at the facility.

4. Schedules the hours members will work, and supplies a cashbox and change.

5. Prices any items that are not marked and sees that the prices are realistic.

6. Makes certain sales tax is collected if required.

7. Arranges for freezer storage of leftovers, or cuts prices in half toward close of sale.

8. Turns profit over to treasurer.

9. Thanks all workers and donors.

RUMMAGE SALE

Small rummage sales where members collect donations from themselves and friends and sell the items at a local flea market or member's home are easy to do. Depending upon the amount and quality of donations, the sale can net several hundred dollars. A sale at a house has to be advertised, and signs should be posted at nearby corners. The only expense at a flea market is the cost of renting space.

A large rummage sale can make a great deal of money, sometimes thousands of dollars, but holding one requires a great deal of hard work over many months. It should be attempted only if the members are willing to devote the time and effort.

Committees Needed: General chairperson, donation, storage, transportation, sorting and pricing, setup or equipment, cashiers, cleanup.

Place: A rented store, community center, church or fraternal hall, civic auditorium, or school can be used depending upon the organization's purpose and ability to pay. Things to check on are capacity of building, fire regulations, insurance, rest rooms, and parking space.

Contract: The price, date, hours, and all essential details must be included.

Date: An early fall date is best. It is unwise to get too close to Christmas or into bad weather.

Storage of Rummage: This is the biggest problem. To hold a sale resulting in a net profit of several thousand dollars, a great deal of rummage must be collected. It must also be stored. A church-affiliated organization may be able to use a vacant room in the church hall. Fraternal organizations and women's clubs often own buildings where donations can be stored. Other groups will have to ask members to store the rummage in attics, basements, and garages. The general chairperson or the donations chairperson makes arrangements for this. The donations committee needs workers who can pick up rummage from donor's homes. Trucks must be available to transport donations to the facility the day or night before the sale.

Publicity: This must be started months before the sale, to alert the community that the organization is collecting rummage and should intensify before the date, so that the public will come and buy. Besides newspaper stories, posters and paid advertising may be necessary. (See "Public Relations," Chapter XIV.)

Sorting and Pricing Committee: This should be a large committee, so that no one has to work too many hours. Rummage should be sorted into men's, women's and children's clothing, kitchenware, dishes, small appliances, books, linens, bedding, jewelry, shoes, knickknacks, pictures and frames, etc. The sorters should feel free to discard soiled or damaged items. Broken glass in picture frames should be removed.

One or two members of the committee must be knowledgeable about pricing jewelry, old books, collectibles, and antiques. These are sold at a special treasure or collectibles booth or table. Other items can be priced from 10¢ to $5 or more. The pricers must remember to keep prices low. The object of the sale is to sell the merchandise.

Setup or Equipment Committee: This committee plans the physical setup of the sale. Members may have to borrow or rent tables and erect booths. There must be adequate aisle space, so the public can walk between the tables. An arrangement of four tables in a square, with two people working inside, to straighten merchandise and keep an eye on it, is ideal.

The public should be limited to two or three exits, where cashiers' tables are located. Remember to keep fire exits clear.

Cashier Committee: One member is in charge to answer all questions and to collect money from the cashboxes at regular intervals and deposit it. This money should not be kept overnight in anyone's house. A decision must be made ahead of time about accepting checks. A cash-only policy is best.

The cashiers will need paper sacks and wrapping material, receipt books, adding machines, and sales tax charts (if required).

Pilferage: There is almost no way to prevent this at a large sale. Jewelry and small antiques can be kept in a glass display case and sold directly from that table. The receipt gets the customer past the checkout table. There may be a booth at the entrance where customers are asked to leave shopping bags, or a sign posted asking them not to take them inside the room. Most people are honest, but some stealing will take place at a rummage or flea market sale. The best way to prevent this is to minimize the use of booths that limit vision, and have plenty of help available. Switching of price tags can be expected if peel-off labels are used. This is not as easy if, where possible, stringed price tags are used instead.

Actual Conduct of the Sale:

1. The public must not be allowed inside until the advertised time for the doors to open.

2. The general chairperson or cochairperson must be available at all times, to answer questions or make decisions.

3. A firm policy regarding offers should be decided ahead of time.

4. The cashiers and workers must be given breaks.

5. Some organizations will take markdowns or accept half price toward the end of the day. This should not be announced ahead of time, because customers will collect boxes of merchandise and wait for markdown time.

Lost and Found: This can be handled by the cashiers, or at a special booth where information about the organization is disseminated.

Cleanup Committee: These members straighten the building, pack leftover merchandise and transport it to storage or to a second-hand dealer or charitable organization that has agreed to accept it, and return all borrowed equipment.

Final Duties of General Chairperson: At the end of the sale, the chairperson tallies the receipt books, counts the remaining money, and totals the deposit slips with the cashier chairperson. All money taken in should show on receipt books or cash registers rented or borrowed for the sale. If sales tax is collected, it is shown separately. Some discrepancy will probably result, but the chairperson should remember that the members are not professional salespeople and that mistakes are to be expected.

The general chairperson pays any state or local sales tax and the rent for the building, if this has not been paid in advance. All profit is turned over to the treasurer with a full report on expenses.

WINE-TASTING AND ARTS-AND-CRAFTS FAIR

Especially on the West Coast and in states where wine is made, wine-tasting in conjunction with an art show or an arts-and-crafts fair has become popular and profitable. A Saratoga, California, non-profit group has raised money this way, to provide scholarship funds, pay the salary of a music teacher, provide for vision-screening, and build a wooden climbing structure for the play yard of a preschool.

Committees Needed: Cochairpersons are in charge of the event. Committees needed are wine, art, food, tickets, hostess, decorations, raffle, cleanup, public relations, and program.

Wine: Donations of wine are solicited from area wineries. These donations to a nonprofit, tax-exempt group are tax-deductible, and many wineries will cooperate because of the good will and because their wines will be listed and explained in the programs handed to each guest. A two- to three-paragraph history of the winery, its address, and the hours that it is open to the public, are included.

If additional wine is needed, it is purchased from a local liquor store at a discount or at a winery. The liquor store will lend glasses if the wine is purchased there. Ice or refrigeration is needed.

Food: Food is usually donated by the members. It consists of finger foods suited to accompanying wine and, if kitchen facilities are available, may include some hot tidbits. Members are asked to donate several plates of their specialties and to supply a dozen recipe cards for each one.

Art: A show where area artists and craftspeople display and sell their work can be held with the wine-tasting. Artists are invited to participate and are charged a fee for their space. A percentage of sales over a minimum amount is asked, as a donation to the organization.

A committee may be appointed to jury both the art and the crafts, so that the material displayed is of professional quality. Standards include originality (no kits or copies of work, or ceramics made in molds), how well the article is assembled, quality of workmanship, balance of line and form, appropriate use of color and materials, and finished appearance. All craft items should be the product of the person entering them. Commercial merchandise should be barred.

Hostesses are needed to pass refreshments and sell recipe cards. Several people are assigned to pour wine.

Raffle: Items to be raffled are solicited from local merchants, who are thanked in the program. Raffle tickets are sold during the event; the raffle is held half an hour before closing.

Decorations: With displays of arts and crafts to attract patrons, decorations can be kept to a minimum. Only the tables where wine is served will need decorating. We suggest paper tablecloths, because of the danger of stains. Since this kind of event can attract 300 to 500 people, at least five wine tables should be spaced about the building to prevent long lines.

Publicity: Posters, flyers, newspaper stories, and advertisements are used. Be sure to include information on where to obtain tickets.

Tickets: The charge is usually $3.50 to $5. The chairperson arranges for printing and distribution of tickets. Each member is asked to try to sell a certain number of tickets. It is important to have enthusiastic membership support of this event, because a large advance-ticket sale is necessary. Tickets are also sold at the door.

Cleanup Committee: This committee returns all borrowed equipment. Charges for a custodian on the weekend are at time and a half, so anything this committee does, such as sweeping and returning tables and chairs to their proper positions, will help reduce this charge.

Place: A community center with large grounds and good parking is ideal. Some of the arts-and-crafts booths may be set up outside, in order to avoid crowding the building.

Date and Time: 3:00 to 5:00 P.M. on a Saturday or Sunday afternoon in the spring or early fall is best.

Warning: Be sure to check regulations regarding the serving of alcoholic beverages in your area.

Chapter XVI

Planning a Convention

People in the professions, people with cultural interests, people with hobbies, and people concerned with improving conditions, are but a few of the many who attend conventions every day. They go to learn new methods, new facts, and new approaches to their professions. The convention brings people together from all parts of the country, even from all parts of the world. The language of the convention is a mutual tongue because of shared interests.

It is through participation in some convention activities, whether in workshops, in the business of the convention, or in serving on a committee or as a delegate, that the member meets people with whom like interests can be shared. More often than not, this also results in lasting friendships.

It is an honor to be selected as a delegate to a convention. The delegate should take careful notes of important meetings and try to share the stimulation and excitement of the convention with members who could not attend.

The convention provides an opportunity to talk with officers of the organization and to learn something more about their proposed programs and objectives. It brings the membership together to formulate policy, hold elections, and share ideas. It is a time to express the concerns of the branches, as well as those of an individual, regarding the purposes and conduct of the business of the organization. Constructive changes can be initiated during this period.

Many activities for pleasure, as well as those for sharing ideas, will be scheduled. Most always, there are so many that choices are inevitable. Members should choose wisely, to get the most out of the convention without exhausting themselves.

Because a state or national convention involves scheduling activities for hundreds—many times, thousands—of people, careful and detailed planning is essential.

Convention Site: Usually the site is chosen two to four years in advance. The following items must be considered before making the selection.

1. Would members have to travel great distances?
2. Is suitable transportation available?
3. Would the cost of transportation tend to keep members away?
4. Are there desirable convention accommodations?
5. Does the exhibition hall meet the organization's needs?
6. Are there places of interest in the city or nearby for possible tours?
7. Is there a convention bureau to give assistance?
8. Is child care available if members want to make attendance an occasion for a family vacation?

The Convention Chairperson is appointed by the president, with the approval of the executive board, immediately after installation. The person selected should have executive and organizational ability and a good sense of finance. The chairperson should be easy to get along with, flexible enough to be willing to change plans to improve on them, yet firm enough to take command of any situation.

A Cochairperson is usually needed to assist with the many responsibilities such a large undertaking entails. This person should be appointed by the chairperson, in consultation with the president and with the approval of the executive board. Residence in the convention city is advisable for both chairpersons, because distance can cause difficulty in initiating and completing plans.

Theme of the convention is chosen by the chairperson, in consultation with the president, at the earliest possible time, because the choice will affect much of the planning. It should be suitable to the purposes of the organization, have general appeal, and be easily carried out throughout the convention. The theme title should be short, an attention-getter, and should stimulate members to attend. For example: an electronics association might choose "Electronics of the Future."

Selection of the Hotel: Accommodations must be looked into with the organization's needs in mind, as well as the comfort of members and guests attending the many functions of a convention. The chairperson should visit at least three hotels to determine which one offers the best facilities and menus. This should be done immediately after appointment, because most good convention hotels require reservations a year or more in advance. The following points should be considered.

1. Transportation to and from airports, bus terminals, and trains.
2. Are there nearby parking facilities for those who come in cars?
3. Is there a physician on call and within easy reach?
4. Is there a nurse in the hotel?
5. Is there a barber and/or beauty shop in the hotel?
6. Is there a pharmacy in the hotel?
7. Does the hotel have a coffee shop?
8. What impression does the lobby make?
9. What special rates for rooms are offered for the convention?
10. What guarantees must the organization make for the number of rooms occupied and the numbers for each meal?
11. In case of cancellation, what is the deadline, and if there is a penalty, what is it?

Once these questions have been answered, it is time to discuss the organization's needs with the conventions' department of the hotel. The chairperson will want to do the following:

1. Look over the rooms offered for guests.
2. Look over rooms for the president and the convention chairperson. These are usually complimentary suites.
3. Look over space for registration tables.

4. Inspect accommodations for a boutique sale.

5. See the hall or large room offered for business meetings.

6. Inspect the space allotted for elections. It should have an entrance and an exit at opposite ends of the room if possible, and a lavatory for the use of the election committee. There should be some provision made for bringing meals to the committee, because they may not leave the election quarters until the final count has been made.

7. Decide whether the rooms offered for workshops will be large enough to accommodate those in attendance.

8. Have a place allotted in the lobby for the group's information booth.

9. See if there is a stage and dressing rooms, if they are necessary for the program.

10. Check the acoustics and the sound equipment, to be certain that everyone will be able to hear distinctly from all parts of banquet and meeting rooms.

11. Check on tables, to learn the number seated at each one, and whether they are round or oblong, in order to know how the centerpieces should be designed.

12. Ask to see the colored cloths and napkins, to decide which ones would be suitable for each banquet.

13. Find out what kind and what color, as well as how long, the skirts for the head tables are.

14. Find out the lengths of the platforms for the head tables, to determine how many can be seated at those tables.

15. Find out if the hotel has available such things as large candelabra or other special lighting, and whether its use would be complimentary or what the charges would be.

16. Discuss the cost for each separate meal, whether gratuities and tax are included, and what guarantees must be made, and by what date, as well as the deadline for any cancellations.

17. Sample a meal at each hotel.

18. Find out if the food for banquets is prepared in the hotel's kitchens or is catered by an outside firm. If the food is catered, sample a meal.

Report to Executive Board: The conventions chairperson presents complete information on the prices of rooms, meals, and any extra charges, and makes a recommendation as to which of the hotels is best. The executive board approves this recommendation, subject to approval of the convention committee and the officers who will attend the first convention planning meeting.

Approval of Convention Committee: At the same board meeting, the conventions chairperson asks for approval of the members of the conventions committee. The committee is composed of the following chairpersons, each of whom will need workers to help them carry out their duties: budget, program, workshops, tours, hospitality, decorations, contests (if applicable), exhibition, boutique (if one is planned), registration, courtesy, public relations, elections, awards, and printing. Job descriptions, and other pertinent information necessary for the convention objectives should be given to the chairpersons at the time of appointment. With these as a guide, members of the committee can arrive at the first meeting, prepared to share creative ideas effectively. (See "Planning a Convention," Chapter XVI.)

First Meeting of the Convention Committee: The convention chairperson conducts this meeting, which should be held at the hotel, so that the committee can inspect the facility. In addition to the cochairperson and the convention committee, the president, treasurer, recording secretary (to take the minutes), and corresponding secretary (to handle special correspondance) are invited to attend. The date should be carefully chosen, so that all members can be present.

Agenda:

1. Roll call.
2. Tour of the facility. Committee members should take note of space, storage, seating arrangements, stage, platforms, exits and entrances, etc., so that the best rooms are chosen for each activity.

Lists should be compiled now, so that all requirements for each committee and activity in the room chosen are ready to put into the agreement with the hotel. Three copies should be made, one for the hotel, one for the convention chairperson, and one for the committee head.

3. Contract. The agreement with the hotel can now be completed and prepared for the signature of the president and recording secretary, if the convention committee approves the facility. The agreement should include all details regarding assigned rooms, complimentary suites, complimentary rooms for activities and banquets, guarantees and deposits. The cost of meals, and whether this price covers gratuities and tax, must be in the contract. The menu for each meal must be listed as well. When planning the menus, the chairperson should remember that people attending from out of the area will appreciate a chance to sample regional delicacies.

4. Presentation by the convention chairperson of the convention theme and an overview of the convention, including the numbers of breakfasts, luncheons, and dinners that will be part of the convention package; special functions such as receptions, exhibits, and tours; hours allotted for workshops and demonstrations; and hours for the membership to meet as a whole to conduct business.

5. Presentations by the convention-committee chairpersons of their plans, with estimates of costs and any special equipment required.

6. Creative discussion and recommendations by the committee members, to avoid duplication of effort and to promote plans for a stimulating convention can take place at this time.

Finances:

1. Budgeted funds for the various committees must be taken out of organization money. All committee heads need to know that their budget requirements can be met before completing plans. Consideration should be given to all written budgets and requests for advance funds where needed, and presented to the executive board for approval.

2. Convention operating fund covers the costs of fees for guest

speakers, special entertainment, printing, mailing, extra food or re-
ception costs, flowers, corsages, fruit baskets, telephone, and mis-
cellaneous other expenses.

3. Registration fees and sums added to the charge for meals can
defray these operating costs. Careful consideration of these possible
expenses should be made when setting the charges for registration
and meals.

4. Exhibition fund: An entry or rental fee may help cover the cost
of the exhibition hall. Judges' fees, the catalogue and program-print-
ing costs, photographic coverage and mailing may have to be ab-
sorbed by the organization.

5. Award fund: This is set up if contests for members are a part of
the convention activity. A group of poets or artists might have such a
contest. Certificates for special services to the organization are often
awarded by the president and chairpersons. Printing of these citations can come out of this fund or out of organization money.

6. A boutique sale is one way to get some extra money. This
activity can be counted on to bring in a sizable sum because it is
practically all profit—all merchandise is donated by members.

Additional Duties of the Convention Chairperson:

1. Coordinate the work of all committees. If possible, the chairperson or cochairperson should sit in on planning sessions of these
committees.

2. Establish deadline for printing requirements, and approve the
copy for the convention program.

3. See that invitations to the convention are sent to the President
of the United States, the governor of the state, the mayor of the city,
and any honorary members of the organization.

4. Preside at the convention to introduce the officers, guests,
speakers, and program, unless the rules or protocol determine otherwise. (There is a tendency to eliminate long receiving lines and other
formalities, which take up much valuable time.) Frequently the
chairperson of a particular event serves as the presiding officer.

5. Troubleshoot. Even with the best planning in the world, things
will go wrong. A speaker may have to cancel at the last second,

scarcity of an item will necessitate a menu change, or a committee head may become ill. The chairperson should be flexible enough to change plans at the last minute, if necessary. If the hotel does not live up to its contract, perhaps by serving an inferior meal, an adjustment should be requested of the management.

6. Final report. Reports of all committee heads are compiled into the general report of the convention by the convention chairperson. One copy is for the president, one for the recording secretary, and one for the next convention chairperson.

Chapter XVII

Duties of the Convention Committees

The activities of the convention are planned and carried out by the convention committees. It is important that there be no omissions that could prevent the convention from running smoothly. The following list specifies the duties of most committees needed for a convention. Other duties and other chairpersons will probably have to be added for the particular needs of various organizations. It is essential to select responsible, dedicated chairpersons.

The Budget Committee: This Committee should review the convention budgets of previous administrations to determine approximately what allowances will be required by each committee. Inflation must be considered in estimating costs. Tentative budget needs of each committee should be requested before the first planning meeting, in order to estimate the probable total cost of the convention. The charge for registration for members and guests should be set to cover costs of running the convention. Costs of business conducted at the convention, such as printing of the minutes should come out of organization funds. The budget and registration fee must be approved by the executive board.

Publicity for Conventions: This is discussed in "Public Relations," Chapter XIV.

The Printing Committee: This committee is in charge of all material that has to be printed for the convention. Each committee chairperson should submit exact copies and the required numbers of all printing that must be done to the printing chairperson as early as possible. Three bids must be obtained for printing. Quality as well as price must be a consideration. The printer should be reliable and be able to make last minute changes and corrections if that becomes necessary. The printing committee should include an artist capable of designing program covers and doing layout to save on costs. The organization's logo and the convention theme title should be used on programs and folders. The usual committees requiring printing are:

1. Registration: tickets in different colors for each function and meal, copies of convention rules, badges, the convention program, registration forms, folder to hold convention material.

2. Public relations: brochures, advance copies of speeches.

3. Program: individual programs for each banquet or other form of entertainment.

4. Workshops: material related to the workshops.

5. Exhibition: program, catalogue, ribbons (if awards are made).

6. Hospitality and courtesy committees: badges.

7. Tour: registration forms, brochures.

8. Awards: certificates for citations of service.

9. Some organizations hold a memorial service for deceased members at the time of the convention. This service would require a printed program.

The Exhibition Committee: If there is to be an exhibition in connection with the convention, arrangements must be made early, in order to secure a suitable hall for the dates required. The exhibition may consist of the members' work (an art show or flower-arranging demonstration, for example) or it may be display booths set up by manufacturers to demonstrate their products and educate conventiongoers to technological advances in their fields. In deciding upon the exhibition hall, the following items should be considered:

1. Is the hall large enough to house the anticipated exhibits?

2. Does the hall have proper and sufficient lighting for displays?

3. Are there display tables, locked glass cases, shelves, etc? Is there seating?

4. Is there a storage area where exhibits can be unpacked and repacked for shipment?

5. Is there storage available for delivery of exhibits, and, if not, how close is the nearest warehouse? If necessary, warehouse costs and facilities should be checked.

6. Insurance coverage for theft, fire, loss through breakage or other damage, and liability to cover injury to workers or guests must be investigated.

7. If refreshments are planned, will the hall cater them? If not, can the organization hire a caterer or handle the refreshments itself?

8. Are kitchen facilities available, and what are the rules for use of the equipment? Are the dishes and serving pieces adequate? What is the responsibility for accidental damage or breakage?

Contract: Approval of the executive board is necessary.

Duties of the exhibition committee are many, so a fairly large one is needed to attend to the following:

1. Decide on the rules for the exhibitors.

2. Decide on judges and the rules by which the judges shall select the winners if awards are made.

3. Decide what honorarium or other gift to give to judges.

4. Send the rules to the judges chosen, and arrange for the date and time for judging.

5. See that the rules for exhibitors appear in the house organ or newsletter early in the administration, or notify manufacturers so they can make advance plans.

6. Be sure rules include that cost of repacking and of returning exhibits must be included with the fee and application.

7. Plan how the exhibit should be set up and the times, hours, and days each member would need to work.

8. If special exhibits require novel displays, it may be necessary to order them or to have some members assemble them. (For example, a garden committee put a waterfall together, to enhance a display of

fuchsias.) Cost, sturdiness, and ease of disassembling and/or transportation could be a factor in deciding whether to order such a
display.

9. Consider costs of storage before exhibits are delivered to the
hall.

10. Accept delivery between certain stated hours at a specified
place if the exhibit consists of members' work. The members' work
could be delivered by the members themselves. If paintings, weaving, jewelry, sculpture, or other articles are shipped to the convention city, the committee members will have to receive and unpack
exhibits and check them immediately for any damage or loss. These
members are responsible for delivering the exhibits to the hall, returning them to the packing area, and seeing that they are repacked
and shipped back to the owner. Any charges over the sum sent for
return should be billed to the owner.

11. Take down the exhibit. If the exhibits are massive or heavy,
the committee members must be able to handle them, or they must
hire help. Money to take care of this expense must be budgeted.

12. Make security arrangements to protect valuable exhibits.

13. Welcome guests, and hand out programs and/or catalogues
during the exhibit.

14. Arrange for and serve simple refreshments, if these are necessary.

Awards, if there are any, are given at a special banquet. Winners
should be informed in time for them to be present, if possible. It is a
courtesy to invite the judges to be present also.

The Program Committee: Much of the program should be decided
upon by this committee, the convention chairperson, and the president. The program should be planned around the theme of the convention. It is customary to have a speaker address the group on some
subject related to its purposes after most of the meals. Music is often
used as a background for receptions and receiving lines. Sometimes
the members of an organization wish to present a program demon-
strating its goals or activities. The program chairperson should encourage and help the group with their planning. Before making

commitments for programs, the chairperson should confer with the budget chairperson. (See "Duties of Other Officers," Chapter V for help with planning programs.)

Workshops: These are an important addition to any convention. It is essential that the workshops be carefully planned, taking into consideration the interests and goals of the members. Workshop leaders should be invited to present workshops at least a year in advance. Subject matter should be discussed in detail and an outline requested for use in publicity releases.

Members can serve as workshop leaders, serve on panels, or as speakers for special programs. Demonstrations of techniques and the use of new materials can trigger the creative juices.

A workshop can be set up to do something about a particular problem. Organized into small groups, members spend twenty minutes or more picking one another's brains. One of the group is chosen to report on the collective response to the problem. In a fairly large convention, there may be many groups of this kind, each of which will present their solutions. Usually, out of these there will be:

1. a number of similar solutions
2. a decision to act upon one of these recommendations
3. a committee set up to investigate further
4. a date set for the committee report and a decision for further action
5. a solution that is usually found appropriate to the cause.

Try not to schedule workshops concurrently. At times this can't be avoided. Because convention-goers resent missing something that might interest them, we suggest that appropriate workshops be combined or that panels be set up to cover the subjects.

Duties of the Tour Director: This chairperson makes arrangements for any buses that will be needed in the programming of the convention. If, for example, a memorial service is scheduled in a church two miles from the hotel, arrangements will have to be made to bus members there.

In addition, the tour director should make recommendations to the convention chairperson of tours to places of local interest. For example, persons attending a convention in Washington, D.C., might find the combination bus/boat tour to Mount Vernon exciting, especially if they belonged to an organization interested in the preservation of historic buildings.

If the organization decides to sponsor a post-convention tour to a distant location, the director plans it with a travel agent, arranges all details, and brings an agreement to be signed after approval of the executive board.

Once the tours are decided upon, the information and price (and any extra costs such as admissions and meals) are included on the registration forms. Tour tickets are paid for in advance with the registration fee.

The committee to help the tour director need not be large. It will be necessary to collect tickets as members enter the busses. It is the duty of the committee members to check that every seat is filled, to see that no one is left behind when returning, and to thank the driver.

The Registrations Committee: This committee should meet well in advance of the convention to arrange the details of the following:

1. Tickets. Each ticket must be numbered, and tickets for each function should be a different color. The place, date, and time of the function, the title of the function, and the price must be printed on each ticket.

2. Registration forms. These should include the theme of the convention, the place, address, dates, tours, a list of the functions, with prices for each and as a package deal, and the deadline for registration by mail. The design and information contained in the form must be approved by the convention chairperson, the president, and the executive board.

Registration forms and full details about the convention must be mailed to each member or published in a house organ sent to each member.

SAMPLE REGISTRATION FORM

THE BLANK HOTEL, MIAMI, JANUARY 11-13, 1980

"Making Tomorrow Brighter"

FRIDAY, JANUARY 11

3:00 P.M.	Executive Board Meeting		
10:00 A.M. to	Registration: Lobby Registration fee	$25.00	___
6:00 P.M.			
8:00 P.M.	Get-acquainted Party	2.00	___
	Exhibits, Book Fair		

SATURDAY, JANUARY 12

8:00 A.M. to			
10:00 A.M.	Registration: Lobby		
10:00 A.M.	New Products Workshop		
11:00 A.M.	Reception for Officers, Awards Judges, and Honored Guests		
11:30 A.M.	Photography Brunch: Speaker, Dr. Ruth Watts, "Photography and the Law"	10.50	___
2:00 P.M.	Copyright Workshop		
3:00 P.M.	Composition Workshop		
4:00 P.M.	Developing-Technique Workshop		
7:00 P.M.	Awards Banquet: Speaker, Thomas Williams, "Photography as Art"	15.00	___

SUNDAY, JANUARY 13

8:00 A.M.	Opportunity Breakfast: Speaker, Nan Jones, "Get Rich Quick"	7.00	___
9:00 A.M.	Equipment Workshop		
10:00 A.M.	Photojournalism Workshop		

1:00 P.M.   Farewell Luncheon: Speaker, James   12.00 ___
             Wilson, "Photography of the Future"

                              Complete Package $72.50 ___

Mail Registration Form, with events checked, with check made
out to "South and West Photographers Convention" to:
Jane Blank, Cochairperson   Enclosed is my check for _____
1111 West Davis Street
City, State 00000

Name _____

Address _____

Registration must be received by December 1, 1980

SAMPLE HOTEL RESERVATION FORM

    To: James F. Brown
    Blank Hotel
    1700 Ocean Drive
    Miami, FL 00000

Please reserve the following room (which I have circled) for:

Name _____

Address _____

Arrival Date _____ Hour _____ Date Departing _____

DESIRED ACCOMMODATIONS AND RATE

Single (One Person)	$30	$33	$36
Double (Two People)	$45	$48	$60
Suite (Parlor, Two Bedrooms Four People)	$150	$160	$170

   3. Folder to hold convention material.
   4. Ribbon badges needed by all officers, both of the convention
chairpersons, candidates for office, pages, committee chairper-

sons, and members. They will be needed for identification. This avoids confusion. For example: people without proper identifying badges would not be permitted to handle exhibits, to decrease the chance of loss or irreparable damage.

Registration committee members who will actually be at the registration desks must meet in advance of the convention, to be informed of procedure and to set up assignments. As soon as the printing and other material to be inserted is available, the committee makes up the packets. These will be filed in alphabetical order as the registrations are received. There should not be too many packets for each person to handle at registration time. No one should be expected to be on duty all day.

Registration Packets: They may be contained in a special folder designed for that purpose or in a large manila envelope. There should be space on the back of the folder for the following:

1. Name of registrant and title (also note if he or she is a candidate, member of a committee, etc.)

2. Branch or chapter (if that applies).

3. Address and phone number.

4. Registration number.

5. The number of tickets. List each function and price.

6. Amount of check and bank and check number.

7. The number of the account sheet where the check is recorded in the account book.

Packet should contain:

1. Copy of convention rules.

2. Envelope containing tickets. Name and room number should be on back of tickets.

3. Name badge and, where needed, identifying ribbons. The badge should give name, title, and branch or chapter.

4. Program and other printed material, as selected by the committee for convention use.

5. Notebook or pad and pencil are a nice courtesy.

6. A city map, with locations of exhibits and other activities not at the hotel circled.

A master list of numbers of members making reservations for

each function and meal must be compiled for the convention chairperson.

Extra tickets, exchanges of tickets, lost tickets, and all other ticket requirements, outside of those already in the packets, should be handled by one person, to save time and avoid confusion. Sales of extra tickets for reserved meals or other functions must be reported to the convention chairperson, who will inform the hotel of the additions. It should be emphasized that after the deadline, no refunds will be made. This is necessary to maintain banquet or other guarantees.

Checks can be deposited to a special convention account. Technically this money is not a part of the organization's funds, so setting up a special account does not violate the bylaws. The convention's bills would then be paid by the convention chairperson and cochairperson. Two signatures must be on the account and on each check. A complete report of receipts and expenses, including bank statement, must be made to the executive board at the end of the covention.

If checks are sent to the organization's treasurer for deposit, bills for convention expenses will have to go to that officer for payment.

Report: At the end of the convention, the account sheets should be photocopied. A copy goes to the convention chairperson for inclusion in the convention report. The report should include a list of expenditures made by the committee in carrying out its duties.

The Decorations Committee: This committee should meet early, to plan and make samples of table decorations and favors for the many functions of the convention. Designs should be approved by the convention chairperson. Colors must be chosen carefully, to coordinate with the colors of tablecloths and napkins. The convention theme and logo of the organization should be used whenever possible.

This committee should be large enough so that, after all the designs are approved, each individual function will be handled by a separate group of people, who will make the decorations, deliver them to the hotel, and put them on the tables at the proper time. In this way, the committee members will not be overworked. These groups are also responsible for removing the decorations after each function. Arrangements may be made to use the decorations as prizes, by hiding a number at each table.

Either the committee chairperson, or someone designated for that duty, should supervise the placement of decorations at the head table. Favors, place cards, seating arrangements, and all other things necessary at the head table should be handled by that person.

The Hospitality Committee: This committee needs to be large enough to take tickets for meals and other functions. The members should be assigned the times they will be serving. It is their responsibility to welcome guests and escort guests and speakers to their places on the receiving line, at the head table, or in other reserved seating.

The Courtesy Committee: This should be fairly large, because the members will serve in many capacities. There should be an overlap of scheduling so that someone is always available. The committee should meet well in advance of the opening of the convention, to learn what procedures will be necessary and to receive assignments.

1. The information booth must have someone in attendance during convention hours.

2. There should be a telephone in the booth. Telephone numbers of a hospital, ambulance, doctor, nurse, pharmacy, police, and fire departments should be posted.

3. A table with room for maps, convention material and information, and space for lost and found will be needed in the booth.

4. The committee delivers gifts, corsages, baskets of fruit and flowers, and messages, promptly, to the proper people. When flowers cannot be delivered right away, they must be refrigerated.

5. Other members of the committee must see that the American flag, the state flag, and the organization's flags are in the proper places at each function.

7. It is the responsibility of this committee to see that all equipment is in place and in operating order.

8. A water glass and pitcher of water must be at all the speakers' places.

9. The committee should be large enough to leave some members free to help other committees when needed, such as assisting with placement of decorations.

10. Pages are assigned to the president who will direct them in their duties. It may be necessary to have several pages.

The Awards Committee: This committee will need help with direct mail requests for money for exhibition and contest awards. People will be needed to stuff envelopes. The chairperson should publicize the fact that donors of awards will be listed in the convention program and urge that donations come in early, so that the names can be included. The requests can be made through the newsletter or house organ, early enough to allow for a second request, and sometimes a third if it seems necessary.

Awards certificates are ordered through the printing committee by the awards chairperson, who sees that the president has them in ample time to sign each one before the convention. The number needed should come from the president, the convention chairperson, and other people who are responsible for presenting award certificates for outstanding service to the convention or the organization.

The Contest Committee: This committee should review contests in "Special Events," Chapter XVIII. Winners should be notified in time, so they can be present at the convention to receive their awards. The names of winners should be given to the public relations chairperson, so that information can be forwarded to the local papers in the community where the winner resides. A list of winners and the categories should be sent to the editor of the house organ for inclusion in that magazine. Entrance fees should have covered all expenses. These contests are for members only.

Duties of the Boutique Committee:

1. The chairperson should live in the convention city, or appoint someone living there, to accept and store donations.

2. Donations should be requested in the newsletter early enough to give members time to create something for the sale.

3. Donors should be listed in the convention program, if possible, or thanked at one of the convention banquets.

4. Donations should be entered in a book with columns headed with "item and number," "donee," "acknowledged," "price," and "sold." If two people are logging in donations a letter is added to the item number in the second book—example; 12A.

5. If antiques and art are among the things donated, someone knowledgeable about current prices should be asked for advice.

6. Equipment needed: a cash box that can be locked, a glass display case for valuable small items that can be locked, a rack for clothing items, if they are expected, and hangers for the clothing, tags, preferably with string for attaching (removable adhesive tags sometimes come off too easily causing confusion), receipt books with carbons, an inventory book or books, a stapler, pens (one red one), tissue papers, paper bags (ask committee members to save them), and boxes in which to pack the donations after they are priced.

7. The sales room in the hotel should be large enough to hold the donations without crowding. It will need to have ample storage space in a closet or closets, and display cases and tables.

During the sale itself, the points listed below should be followed:

1. The committee should be large enough to allow members to take turns at selling. Assignments of days and hours should be made in advance of the convention.

2. Committee members should be given a typed list of instructions for the manner in which the sales, payments, etc., are to be handled.

3. If the hotel will make the room available, the merchandise can be transported a day in advance of the convention, so that it can be unpacked and arranged.

4. One person should be appointed to keep merchandise in order and answer questions. If the public has access, merchandise must be watched carefully.

5. The checkout table at the door should have two people in attendance at all times. One person writes the receipt upon payment. (An adding machine is helpful.) A state sales-tax chart should be handy for reference. The item number, price, and amount of tax

(if it must be charged) go on the receipt. The second person wraps the merchandise and checks it off as sold in the inventory book. Packaging material and the inventory book should be right at hand on a table large enough to do the wrapping.

6. Money: Some cash for change will be needed in the box. A policy regarding the acceptance of checks should be decided upon in advance with the convention chairperson. At night, money collected during the day should be put into the hotel's vault.

7. After the sales, as unsold articles are packed, the number is circled in red in the inventory book, to indicate that they have not been sold. This will complete the inventory.

8. Sales receipts and prices of all sold merchandise from the inventory notebooks are added separately. Then the money is counted. The sums should be equal. The money is turned over to the person handling the convention funds with a statement of how much sales tax must be paid.

9. A flea market is a good place to sell leftover articles. The money is sent to the organization's treasurer.

Duties of the Nominations Committee:

1. If election of officers is a part of the business of the convention, nominations will have been made earlier, according to the rules set forth in the bylaws.

2. The nominations chairperson sends the list of candidates to the elections chairperson at least two months before the convention, so that ballots can be printed.

3. The names of approved nominees are presented verbally by the nominations chairperson at the request of the presiding officer, at the scheduled time during the business meeting, usually the day before elections.

4. It is customary for the president to ask each one to step up before the podium, as the names are called. This gives members an opportunity to see the candidates before the election takes place.

ELECTIONS

Please refer to your bylaws and standing rules for the duties of the election committee, since the rules may vary. Here is one method of electing officers at convention:

Facilities: The room to be used for elections should be chosen at the first planning meeting. Other items that will be needed are tables and chairs for the people who serve as election workers, tables to hold ballot boxes, and a curtained-off area for voting.

Printing Requirements: official branch reports, accreditation cards, ballots, and absentee ballots. See samples.

SAMPLE FORM NUMBER ONE

OFFICIAL BRANCH REPORT

Branch members entitled to vote at the convention.

Name of branch _____ State _____ Total number of voters _____
On or before (date), each branch president must send two (2) copies of this report to the elections chairperson.

GROUP 1—VOTING OFFICERS

Name of branch officers   Office held as of (date)

_____ President—date

_____ Treasurer—date

National officers in the branch:

(Name) _____ (Title) _____

        _____   _____

        _____   _____

GROUP II—ACCREDITED BRANCH DELEGATES

As of _____ , branch treasurer's books show _____ active members in good standing (dues paid up). In the ratio of one delegate to each ten members, this branch is entitled to _____ accredited branch delegates, with an alternate for each delegate. Accredited delegates and alternates are listed as elected by this branch. An individual name may appear only once in this group. No names appearing in Group I can appear in the group listed below. *(If no delegate can attend the convention, mailed-in votes may be sent according to the rules.)*

      Name of Delegate   Name of Alternate

_____   _____

(As many spaces as are judged necessary may be designed.)

           Signed _____ Branch President

                  _____ Date

        Address _____

No accreditation cards and no absentee ballots can be sent to the branch until this form is return to the Elections

Chairperson (Name) _____ (Address) _____

SAMPLE FORM NUMBER TWO

INSTRUCTIONS FOR USE OF ACCREDITATION CARD

These are your accreditation cards (enclosed). They are very important. Remember that delegates must bring them. No one can vote without a card. Each card is exchanged for one ballot. The card must be signed by the branch president and bear the same name as that sent to the elections chairperson.

WAYS TO VOTE

1. Only registered voters may cast a ballot in person while attending the convention. Time for registration is . . . . Accreditation

cards will be checked by the elections committee at the time of registration.

2. If an alternate is to attend the convention and cast the vote, the delegate's card, properly endorsed on the back by the delegate and branch president, must be presented with the alternate's own credentials.

3. Vote by proxy may be made only if the voter is authorized to vote for someone who could not attend. That person's card must be properly endorsed to the voter on the back of the card.

4. Vote by mail may be accomplished by absentee ballot. The number of ballots needed must be requested by the president. The returned ballots must be postmarked no later than one month prior to the convention. Accreditation cards (one for each ballot) must be clipped to the outside of the envelope in which the ballots were sealed. The sealed envelope is enclosed in another envelope and sent to the elections chairperson.

SAMPLE ACCREDITATION CARDS

DELEGATES

Registration number _____

Name _____

Branch _____

No. of accredited votes _____

Signed _____ Pres.

Signed _____ Treas.

ALTERNATES

Registration number _____

Name _____

Branch _____

No. of accredited votes _____

Signed _____ Pres.

Signed _____ Treas.

REVERSE SIDES

Endorsed to _____

By _____

Signed _____ Pres.

Endorsed to _____

By _____

Signed _____ Pres.

Sample of Official Ballot (usually legal size)

No ____   **ORGANIZATION NAME**

Election of officers *(date to date)*

Vote for only one candidate for each office. Mark ballot X. Write in votes for accredited candidates permitted.

President		First Vice-President	
Name, Branch, State	☐	Name, Branch, State	☐
Name, Branch, State	☐	Name, Branch, State	☐

(Add as many officers as are needed.)

Mailing: Mailing of the material and letters pertaining to the election is done by the committee. Form Number One is mailed to branch presidents six months prior to the convention date.

Cards: As the number-one forms are returned by branch presidents, accreditation cards and alternates cards are mailed out with Form Number Two.

Filing:

1. As each letter comes in, it is numbered and filed in loose-leaf binder number one.

2. A cross-index file is set up in loose-leaf binder number two. In this binder, each branch is indexed by state and carries its number from binder number one. The entry includes the name of each president, treasurer, delegate, and alternate.

3. As cards are mailed, or absentee ballots requested, the pages are so marked and dated.

4. When absentee ballots are mailed to those requesting them, the number and date are red-inked in the file.

5. When ballots are returned, the number and date are green-inked on the page.

Rules: Any changes in rules and procedures must have the approval of the executive board in ample time to allow for printing and mailing. Only those procedures that are listed in the standing rules can be changed. Rules that are written into the bylaws can be changed only by amendment.

Registration:

1. As each delegate is registered, the accreditation card must be checked with the file by a member of the elections committee.

2. The card is stamped REGISTERED when checked as accurate.

Election: A member of the committee will exchange the accreditation card for a ballot. The ballot must have the same number as the accreditation card on the upper left-hand corner.

Ballot: As each member is given a ballot, the corner with the number is cut off and put into a special box for that purpose. This is done so the count can be double-checked.

Voting: The voter enters the voting booth to vote. When the voter has completed the ballot, it is folded and put into the sealed election box.

Exit: The voter leaves by exit door. No one may return.

Polls: They must close at the time set by the rules. No one may enter while the count is being made. If the voting membership is fairly large, it may be necessary to have several counters with one person at the blackboard listing the number of votes for each candidate. It is necessary to have a second crew to count again to be certain that the count is accurate.

Poll Watchers: Each candidate is entitled to appoint a poll watcher to observe the voting and counting.

Report: The report of the number of votes for each of the candidates is made up by the elections chairperson.

Results: Should be read at the time prescribed by the convention program, usually the same evening or early the next day. All candidates are mailed the results of the voting. The elected officers receive a formal notice of their election to office from the elections chairperson and a congratulatory letter from the out-going president.

The Public Relations: This chairperson is given the results immediately following the final count.

Finances: Election of officers is a part of the organization's business. Expenses of election are paid for by the treasurer.

REPORTS

At the close of the convention, all convention-committee chairpersons write complete reports of their activity, including financial details. These reports go to the convention chairperson who compiles a complete report of the convention. Copies of this report go to the president and the recording secretary.

Chapter XVIII

Special Events

Along with continuing programs, such as monthly or quarterly meetings with speakers or demonstrations, fund-raisers, supplying volunteer workers, or awarding scholarships to further their objectives, many organizations also plan special events. Generally such projects are in keeping with the group's purpose and the interests of its members. They are sponsored to improve the quality of life in the community and to provide cultural and educational enrichment.

While such events can also be fund raising, usually they are not held for this purpose. Entry fees or admission charges are set to cover only the organization's expenses. Donations can be solicited to help keep down costs. Several groups may cosponsor a large event, such as a spring ecology fair, that can feature exhibits of educational materials, arts, crafts, local bands, singers, tumblers, mime troupes, clowns, food booths, and may kick off with a parade. Literary or art contests, one-day workshops, conferences, seminars, exhibits, athletic contests, arts-and-crafts fairs, and music festivals are among events organizations offer in many communities. The opportunity to view live theater or to attend lectures and concerts would not be possible in many small towns without the devoted work of organizations that bring the artists to the area.

Groups contemplating such projects need to consider the idea carefully. Failure can result in the loss of both money and prestige.

Success depends upon meticulous planning and the availability of dedicated members who will find pleasure and achievement in furthering the goals of the organization and making their community a better place in which to live.

Choosing an Event to Sponsor

1. *Choose carefully.* Careful selection is of utmost importance. The organization must decide whether there is a need for the activity and a potential audience.

2. *Avoid duplication.* If ten art groups already sponsor exhibits in your area, another one only duplicates efforts and dilutes participation of both artists and public.

3. *Join forces.* If your members insist that an art exhibit be an activity of your club, suggest approaching a similar organization with the idea of holding a joint show. It might be possible to expand the exhibit to include such things as sculpture and weaving. Demonstrations and lectures by well-known artists could be an added attraction. Your group's willing workers and added support can lead the way to increased cooperation among the community's organizations.

4. *Be timely.* Make an effort to discover current concerns and interests of people in your area. If your idea is a seminar on money, make it more specific. Should you limit it to investments for retired persons, or should it be for the career woman? Perhaps it should be designed for working couples. Since financial management for women receives a great deal of attention today, your organization's seminar on money might better be slanted to young men who certainly need just as much help with investments as women.

5. *Or be old-fashioned.* Because of the interest in hunting down ancestors, genealogy societies have sprung up across the country, as people unite to share methods and material. The roots of a community, how it started, who were the first inhabitants, what events occurred during its early years are of interest to present-day residents. While many towns in the South and East have historical pageants that celebrate their birth, others completely neglect their history. If your organization's purposes are historical preservation,

community betterment, or education, a project relating to the beginnings of your community should be considered.

6. *Look for a tie-in.* Is your town the artichoke, azalea, or rice capital of the world? Is it famous for redwood trees, salmon fishing, bauxite mining, or Victorian architecture? If you can tie your project to something for which the community is already known, you'll find it easier to arouse interest. Consider also a tie to the calendar. Is there a connection between your event and a holiday? Is it appropriate for Halloween or National Safety Week?

7. *What is the project's purpose?* Does it offer a service or fill an unanswered need? Does local government have the money to clean the beaches and the parks after the tourists go home? Is there a group in your community that takes library books to shut-ins? The pressure to reduce taxes has sharply curtailed government programs in many localities. Can your organization supply the funds or the people needed to put a bookmobile back on the road or to transport children to school?

8. *Is the project worthwhile?* The time and hard work of your members should be used for constructive projects that will be of recreational, cultural, or educational benefit to the community.

9. *Can you do it?* Decide whether it is feasible to hold the event. Does your organization have the finances and personnel to make the project under consideration a success? If there is doubt in members' minds, it might be better to plan a neighborhood fete or a seminar for a limited number of participants. Many neighborhood projects have grown to citywide ones, because the pilot program generated interest and enthusiasm.

Planning Your Project: Conferences, workshops, seminars, and exhibits need the same meticulous planning that is required for a convention. The duties of the general chairperson are much the same. (See Chapters XVI and XVII.) Many of the procedures outlined in "Fund Raising," Chapter XV, will help in organizing a special event.

HOW TO RUN A CONTEST

Contests are held to encourage the development of literary and
artistic talent, to recognize the efforts and achievements of individuals who work to improve their community, and to promote interest
in, and further the objectives of, an organization. For example: an
organization with the purpose of promoting patriotism might sponsor an essay contest for high school seniors on "Why I Am Proud To
Be An American." A camera club might choose to give awards to
outstanding photographs that best depict the spirit of the community.

Selecting the Category: Awards can be made for outstanding land-
scaping, for writing poetry, prose, and music, for the development of
original recipes, for painting, crafts, athletic endeavor, volunteer
effort, and professional achievement. The categories are practically
limitless. Organizations deciding to hold contests should choose a
category that furthers its purposes and falls within the expertise of
its members.

Setting Up the Rules: A committee should be appointed to write the
rules. They should be clear and concise. If a writing contest is held
for children, the rules must state that the entry must be the original
work of the entrant. Young children do not understand the meaning
of plagiarism. To them, an award offered for a "best poem" can
mean the poem they like best. An art contest must specify that no
copy work is allowed.

SAMPLE OF RULES FOR POETRY CONTEST

"The *Pteranodon* poetry contest is open to all poets.
Cash Prizes: 1st place winner will receive $20
                 2nd place winner will receive $10
                 3rd place winner will receive $5

All winning poems and runners-up will be published in the
_____ issue of *Pteranodon*.

Rules: All poems must be original and unpublished.

Poems may be any form, any theme, with a 75-line limit.

A registration fee of $1.00 must accompany each poem.
Send check or money order. Please do not send cash.

Send two clearly typed copies of each poem (full name
and address on one copy of each poem).

Send a self-addressed, stamped envelope for return of
poems and winners list.

All entries must be received no later than _____.

Everything published in *Pteranodon* is copyrighted. The rights
revert back to the author upon publication.

Pteranodon will always have a recognized, respected poet to act
as contest judge. To be completely fair, we will have a different
judge for each contest. The poems are judged anonymously."

Be certain that contest rules include the cut-off date and the address of the person to whom the entries must be sent.

Awards To Individuals: Nominations can be made of individuals
who have contributed greatly to the community, if the organization
decides to make awards to outstanding men and women. Usually an
entry form is printed in the newspaper, although it is possible to
distribute nomination forms through civic organizations, banks, community centers, and libraries.

Sample Nomination Form

I nominate (Name)_____ (Address)_____
for outstanding person of the year.
List five achievements.

1. _____
2. _____
3. _____
4. _____
5. _____

Tell in 25 words or less why you think this person should receive the award. Staple statement to nomination form.

(Your name)_____ (Address)_____

Contest Policy: The contest should not be open to any member of the organization or to a member of that person's family. Many organizations restrict contests they sponsor to amateurs, with the rules prohibiting a person who makes a living as a photographer from entering a camera club's contest.

Entry Fee: Some organizations charge a fee for each entry. This fee is used to pay the judges and to provide money for awards. We do not recommend that fees be charged when the contests are limited to students.

Selection of Judges: Three judges should be chosen. While the organization may use its members as judges, it is customary to select three people from the community who have expertise in the category to judge the entries. For example: a newspaper reporter, the head of an advertising agency, and a college English instructor could be invited to judge an essay contest. The use of outside judges eliminates any possibility that the organization will be criticized for showing favoritism.

Preliminiary Judging: Preliminary screening can be done by a committee of members. All entries that do not adhere to the rules should be eliminated. If there are a large number of entries, the preliminary judging committee can narrow these down to the best 10 or the best 25, thus saving the judges' time.

Publicity: Notice of the contest and the rules must be distributed through newspaper releases and flyers. The names of the winners should be announced. (See "Public Relations," Chapter XIV.)

Judging: Criteria should be established for the judges, and sheets on which they can score the entries should be provided. For an essay contest, originality, appropriate theme, grammar and spelling, and style might be the bases on which the entries are judged. Photographs could be judged on visual impact, composition, contrast, and technique.

Announcing the Winners: The names of the winners can be announced via newspaper release. The names of all winners should be sent to all entrants, upon request and receipt of a self-addressed, stamped envelope.

Presenting the Awards: Awards should be made at a luncheon, dinner, or special meeting of the organization. The winners should have been notified, so that they can be present. Winning art or photographs can be displayed. It is nice to read selections of winning poetry or prose or have winning music played. If the awards are presented at a luncheon or dinner, a table should be reserved for close relatives of the winners.

ORGANIZING A CULTURAL FESTIVAL

Cultural festivals with an old-world flavor can be popular projects. Generally they are two-day affairs, featuring the costumes, music, and foods of an ethnic group. Because they help keep alive the traditions and customs of other cultures, they are educational as well as recreational.

Unless the organization planning to sponsor a cultural fair has a great many members, it is best to ask a number of organizations with related purposes to work together on the project. A general chairperson will be needed to coordinate the effort. Each organization involved should have representatives on the planning committee.

ORGANIZING A CLEANUP OPERATION

If your organization's purpose includes community improvement, a cleanup operation might be a good project. The OP II, One

Planet–One Purpose, organization directs a fall clean-up of the beaches in Santa Cruz and Monterey counties, California. Last year more than 1,000 volunteers cleared 90 tons of debris from 120 miles of coastline during a six-hour effort.

Business, industry, and local government joined forces with the organization, as did groups like the Sierra Club, the Santa Cruz and San Benito Council on Seniors, and the Modified Motorcycle Association. Trucks and four-wheel-drive vehicles were loaned to haul trash to dumps. Volunteer on-beach coordinators directed the removal of litter and broken glass. This project not only saved taxpayer dollars, but also made the beaches safer for area residents.

Success of an operation such as this depends largely upon dedicated members who will make an appeal to other organizations and to the community's business and industrial firms and governmental agencies for the cooperation that is necessary. Since residents of the Santa Clara Valley and the San Francisco Peninsula are heavy users of the beaches, OP II was able to get support from the Intergovernmental Council of Santa Clara County, the Los Gatos Town Council, the Santa Clara County Board of Supervisors, and the San Jose Mercury News, in addition to assistance from local agencies.

Support from area newspapers enabled OP II to get its message out to the volunteer workers that were necessary. However, the project was successful because it gave over a thousand people of all ages an opportunity for exercise and a day at the beach while performing a community service.

Chapter XIX

Special Problems of Community and Tax-supported Groups

Many organizations exist, and more are being formed every day, with the goal of improving the quality of life in a community. A group of citizens may join together to improve nursing-home care, another group may form to promote expansion of the public library, while a third unites to prevent demolition of historically important buildings.

The general membership of these groups can be a cross section of citizens at large from the community who are concerned with services for the elderly, cultural development, preservation of landmarks, educational enrichment, sports opportunities, environmental quality, traffic, safety, or promotion of the arts. They may have both volunteer workers and paid staff. They may interact with city and county employees, boards and commissions appointed by governmental bodies, foundations, elected city, county, and state officials, or all of these.

A parents' club formed at a public school, for example, will work at various times with the principal, the superintendent of schools, and the elected school board. It may also interact with a citizens' committee appointed by the school board to make recommendations on school closures or intercultural education.

Another example of an association that works with various segments of the community is the Friends of the Library. They work directly with the city librarian, but also with a library board appointed by the local governing body. This can be an administrative or advisory board, whichever the charter designates. While the governing body would have the ultimate responsibility for budget and policy, the administration of the library could be by a paid city manager who delegates administrative and personnel affairs to a department head—the city librarian.

Many times such associations are incorporated as nonprofit organizations with membership open to anyone in the community interested in the purposes of the groups. Incorporation can be a requirement for funding. Short-term organizations, such as *ad hoc* citizens' committees appointed by a school board, are usually not incorporated or formally organized because of the expense and the short period of existence.

Finances: Regular dues can be nominal, $1 to $3 a year to attract wide community support and participation. Special membership categories such as patron, sustaining, contributing, and organizational are offered at higher dues, for those who wish to contribute more or who want tax deductions.

These organizations usually engage in fund raising, either through money-making activities or by the solicitation of direct contributions. In addition to this, funds are often obtained from grants or from budget appropriations by a governmental agency for paid staff and office facilities. Support can be solicited from businesses in the community for such activities as mailing a newsletter or making yearly awards to outstanding nursing-home aides.

Financial Records: These organizations must keep careful and complete financial records that meet the standards of the funding agency.

Activity Record: Careful records of each year's activities must be maintained. A summary of these should be provided to the members, paid staff, boards, and applicable governmental or funding agencies. These records should include:

1. *Volunteer effort.* People involved, hours, and job descriptions. Details of volunteer training programs and amount of training offered.

2. *Fund-raisers.* Purpose, attendance, amount raised, cost, and who or what profit was spent on.

3. *Educational effort.* This includes samples of pamphlets published and how distributed, titles of speeches made, by whom and where.

4. *Lobbying.* Appearances before governmental groups and for what purposes.

5. *Membership increase.*

In the case of a grant or tax-supported organization employing professional staff, these records must also include:

1. *Hours of staff work.* This should include the number of hours spent in the office, the number of hours training volunteers, and the number of hours spent on outside investigation.

2. *Telephone calls to office and disposition.* A coded chart should be set up for recording telephone calls. For example: calls made for information that can be provided immediately can be entered on the chart under Column 1. Calls that require the looking up of information and a return telephone call are entered under Column 2. Calls that require outside investigation, such as a visit to a nursing home either by a staff member or a volunteer, are entered under Column 3. Calls that are referred to other agencies are entered in Column 4.

With such a chart, it is easy to total the calls at the end of each month. This record will give the executive board an idea of how well the organization is fulfilling its purpose and is of great value when applying for funding.

3. *The number of outside investigations* by staff or by volunteers and their disposition. In one city, a nursing-home support group received a number of complaints from patients about the food served them. Upon investigation, the professional staff discovered that the

food was indeed poorly prepared. The nursing-home operators were unable to rectify the situation, because they could not find cooks with the necessary experience and training. The executive board of the organization asked the local community college to provide a course for training cooks. The nursing-home operators cooperated by giving their employees time off to attend the classes.

Careful documentation of this kind of problem-solving effort enables an organization to prepare grant and funding applications and gives it an idea of areas where educational effort or additional publicity is needed.

4. *Breakdown of costs per outside investigation.* Keeping track of the number of staff hours involved in handling problems that require outside investigation will show the cost of each one and will help the organization in setting up its budget. These records will also provide the executive board with an insight into staff efficiency.

WORKING WITH THE PROFESSIONAL STAFF MEMBER

Your organization may employ an ombudsman to investigate and resolve complaints by nursing-home patients or their relatives, a manager for a store that sells handicrafts made by senior citizens, or a director to stage plays in the children's theater of the community center. How does the organization's executive board and general membership work with the professional? In what capacity are volunteers used? A clear understanding of what are the organization's policies and what are procedural matters that fall under the expertise of the professional will help the group to function smoothly.

Policy: The Responsibility of the Executive Board.

1. The aims and objectives of the organization as set forth in the bylaws will determine activities recommended by the board.

2. The organization should function according to the rules of order and standing rules. The professional should attend executive board and general membership meetings in an advisory capacity.

3. The board should rely upon the professional's expertise in carrying out procedure.

4. Proper channels of communication for complaints should be established. A member should not go screaming into the professional's office about a situation that he/she thinks was handled improperly. The situation should be brought to the attention of the volunteer coordinator, who takes it to the executive board for investigation. The professional should be brought into the picture at once. Perhaps the complaint is due to a misunderstanding; perhaps the complaint is legitimate, and a procedural change is desirable. However, the fact that a complaint was made merits its investigation.

5. Unless the paid professional is hired for the express purpose of fund raising, he/she should not be involved in asking for contributions to the organization. The professional may be asked to prepare a presentation or write a grant proposal, but should not be required to spend time selling 10 tickets to a dinner. Such fund raising is the responsibility of the members.

6. The staff executive has the responsibility of hiring and firing of paid office staff. The executive board should look for reasons and remedies if there is excessive turnover.

7. The paid professional should never act as the secretary of the executive board. The elected secretary of the organization has the responsibility of taking unbiased and complete minutes and handling board correspondence. The president and the staff executive check the minutes before they are mailed to the other members of the board.

8. The staff executive's salary and performance is evaluated once a year at a meeting at which she/he is not present. The professional is given the results of the evaluation, and any problem areas are discussed.

9. A mutual evaluation is good. The board members should consider whether they have provided the staff executive the support and assistance necessary to carry out the organization's program.

Procedure—the Responsibility of the Staff Executive:

1. Serves as an advisory and resource person to the executive board.

2. Develops and sets up office routine to carry out the organization's objectives in a businesslike manner.

3. Develops a volunteer-training program if the group uses members in a volunteer capacity.

4. Assists the organization's volunteer coordinator to set up standards and schedules for volunteers.

5. Provides the executive board with necessary records and reports. For example: a museum-support group may want to know how many people visited the museum during a month, what acquisitions were made, any special events or exhibits, donations, the number of staff hours worked, the number of volunteer hours worked, and the amount of sales in the gift shop with comparisons to the corresponding month of the previous year.

MAKING A VOLUNTEER PROGRAM WORK

Your volunteer program can be the means by which your organization does a great community service. It can consist of visitors to nursing-home patients, drivers for the ill or elderly, salespeople at senior craft centers or museum gift shops, docents, shelvers and book repairers for the library, storytellers for children's park programs, readers to tape books for the blind, help in the organization's office, and many other wide varieties of social service. In order to get grants or funding from local or state agencies, your group may be required to supply a certain number of volunteer hours. Funding agencies call these "in-kind hours."

For a volunteer program to work successfully, its aims and purposes must be carefully delineated, so that volunteers understand exactly what is expected of them. Careful selection of a volunteer coordinator, who gets along well with people and has the time and energy to devote to this job, is the first step toward success.

DUTIES OF THE VOLUNTEER COORDINATOR

Standards: With the help of the staff executive, the coordinator develops a code for the volunteers. This should be approved by the executive board. Example:

1. Volunteers should wear name tags identifying them as such.
2. Volunteers should never accept recompense or gifts for their services.
3. Volunteers must understand that confidentiality is a prime requisite when dealing with people.

Placement: Volunteers should be carefully placed in various jobs, with a view to best using their talents and experience.

Schedule: Set up a monthly schedule for volunteers, and keep track of the hours each works.

Substitutes: Keep the telephone free a certain time each day, so volunteers who cannot meet their commitments can reach you. Try to have one or two volunteers on call, to fill in for those who must cancel.

Training: Schedule training sessions for volunteers.

Supervision: See that the volunteer has supervision the first couple of times on the job.

Meetings: Schedule meetings for volunteers several times a year, so that problems can be discussed, procedures explained, and volunteer effort evaluated.

SAMPLE VOLUNTEER'S APPLICATION CARD

Name _____ Address _____

Home Phone _____ Business Phone _____

Occupation _____ Where employed _____

Year of birth _____ Place of birth _____

Name of person to notify in emergency _____

Emergency tel. number _____ Education _____

Physical condition _____ Vision _____ Hearing _____

Ages of children at home _____

References (3) _____

Days and hours available per week _____

On reverse of card:

PAST WORK EXPERIENCE			
Type of work	*Where?*	*Paid*	*Vol*

Skills

Arts, crafts _____

Typing _____

Music _____

Other _____

PROBLEM AREAS WITH VOLUNTEERS

Although volunteers work in many educational, cultural, and so-cial-service programs all across the country, there is still some reluctance on the part of paid staff to accept their help, even when the budget is cut so that hours or services will be curtailed without them. The volunteer program should be planned with the help of the staff, and volunteers should not be assigned duties that they are not capable of doing.

Volunteers should not become critical of staff or involved with personnel problems. A volunteer program almost came to an end in one library when a volunteer started criticizing the staff for taking overlong coffee breaks. "Why should we be in here doing hours of hard work when all they do is sit back there and drink coffee and talk?" was the question this volunteer asked several others. The story spread, and the number of volunteer hours dropped. The coordinator investigated and discovered the source of the complaint was an over-long coffee break the children's librarian had taken with the chair-person of the library board. They had discussed the planning of a children's book festival, but had done it over coffee in the lounge instead of in the librarian's office.

Organizations are finding it increasingly difficult to get volunteers, especially with so many women holding full-time jobs. A volunteer program that provides an opportunity for meaningful service and recognition of the volunteer's effort is essential.

Chapter XX

Expansion to State, Regional, and National Level

Far too many organizations struggle alone. People in many areas unite to promote better nursing-home care, solve homeowners' problems, preserve wild rivers, improve the quality of air, fight disease, poverty, or crime. While small groups of hard-working people can and do perform miracles, often far too much effort is spent solving problems that similar groups have already conquered. For such organizations expansion to state, regional, or national level can increase prestige and effectiveness and make it easier to get members.

ADVANTAGES OF EXPANSION

Political Clout: If your organization's purpose is to influence legislation or public opinion, an increase in numbers by the formation of a state association will add weight to your arguments.

Reduced Duplication of Effort: Through newsletters, informational workshops, and seminars, organizations can exchange ideas and learn how other groups have handled similar problems.

Educational Opportunity: Your group will be able to send out information about your purposes and activities to more people.

State Meetings: These will give members an opportunity to talk with outstanding people in their field and develop both friendships and professional contacts.

Better Programs: It is easier to plan programs and attract well-known speakers if you can provide a large audience of interested people.

Better Publicity: A large organization is more apt to get news of its activities into the media than a small one.

HOW TO EXPAND

Through a Former Member: A member who has moved a 100 miles away may encourage people with similar interests to organize and affiliate with your group. While this is a slow method of expansion, the efforts of a devoted and enthusiastic member can result in the formation of an active branch.

Through Friends: Your members can inform friends who live in other areas about the purposes and activities of your group and encourage them to form like organizations affiliated with yours.

Through Existing Groups: You can invite existing groups in other areas that have the same purposes as yours to join in the formation of a state or regional association. These groups can be located by asking chambers of commerce to send lists of organizations in their area, through newspapers, and by consulting the *Cumulative List of Organizations* published by the United States Treasury Department.

HOW TO FORM A STATEWIDE ORGANIZATION

Through Existing Groups:

1. Explore the possibility of state organization, by writing to the presidents of these groups and asking them to consult with their members about a statewide meeting.

2. Appoint a steering committee of members representing the various groups to study the advantages of statewide organization and to write tentative bylaws. (See "Bylaws," Chapter III.) The bylaws committee will have to make recommendations on voting procedure. In a very large organization with many branches, voting can be done by delegates elected by members of the individual branch. This ratio can be 1 delegate per 10 members or 1 delegate per 25 members. Other groups conduct elections by mail, providing each member with a printed ballot. Another method often used is to give each branch or chapter one vote.

3. The steering committee will have to make recommendations as to whether the organization will become a nonprofit corporation. (See "Incorporation," Chapter IX.)

4. Local groups will need assurance that they will not lose autonomy by the establishment of a state or regional association. Local groups will still elect their own officers, plan their own functions and operate under their own bylaws. Local bylaws, however, should not conflict with the proposed bylaws of the state or regional association.

5. Dues to finance the activities of the state or regional association will have to be set. A method of collecting these dues must be established.

6. The proposed bylaws, purposes, and activities of the expanded association should be sent to the existing groups by the steering committee, well in advance of the state meeting, so that local members will have ample time to study them.

7. A time and place for the state meeting must be set so existing groups can gather to vote upon bylaws and election of such officers as called for in the bylaws.

Formation of a New Group: You will need a nucleus of key people scattered throughout the state with energy, organizational ability, and devotion to the purposes and objectives of the proposed association. These key people form a steering committee, contact prospective members, and set up the first meeting.

THE FORMATION OF A NEW NATIONAL ORGANIZATION

It is far easier to organize on the local level and expand slowly over a period of years than it is to jump immediately into national organization. Indeed, this is how most organizations grow.

Before your group decides to try to establish branches in other areas, it might be best to investigate whether there is, already in existence, a national organization doing the same type of work. Affiliation with that one, if possible, could be more advantageous than duplicating and thereby diluting effort.

Almost every trade and profession has its own organization. Nationwide associations for retired people, conservationists, environmentalists, writers, artists, hobbyists, and taxpayers already exist. The Sierra Club, founded in 1892, now has 8,000 local chapters with the purpose of protecting the environment for the enjoyment of future generations. The National Education Association, established in 1857, has over 800,000 members in 2,100 state and local associations, working to get support for public education, and better salaries and working conditions for teachers. The General Federation of Women's Clubs, founded in 1890, now has over 15,000 affiliated clubs and 11,000,000 members in the United States. The first bottle collectors club was organized in 1959. Today there are over 500 bottle collectors clubs in the country. The National League of Americans Pen Women founded in 1897 has over 200 branches in the fifty states.

Organizations with good ideas that are timely and have great appeal to people can spread rapidly across the country and become an effective force. The principles of organizing such groups are the same as forming small, local ones. However, rapid expansion requires the devoted work of many people in various parts of the country and financial backing, for brochures, membership applications and cards, office space, and public relations work.

The organization that spreads slowly, through the efforts of its members and friends, is more apt to be on solid ground, because it will attract members to its already proven programs. The financial outlay will also be less, thereby making lower dues possible.

In 1835 Alexis de Tocqueville wrote, "Americans of all ages, all conditions, and all dispositions constantly form associations." This is true today, as new organizations form and flourish, because of the efforts of dedicated people who know that group action can help solve community problems, thereby enriching its recreational, cultural, and educational climate.

Appendix

At some time, every organization finds it needs more information for the pursuit of its objectives. If it needs help, either financially or otherwise, where does it go for assistance?

Because there are so many different types of associations, no single book can cover all the areas of activity. However, there are ways in which an organization can learn how to get the help it needs.

One of these is through the public libraries. Today, the reference departments of public libraries contain information to satisfy every need. You will find directories that cover activities in the United States and in countries around the world, ranging from ecology to finance. You should find your activities among them. If yours is a beginning organization, you will find others with like interests.

Some have already been listed in the pages of this book. In addition, you may find these useful:

1. *The Encyclopedia of Associations,* edited by Nancy Yakes and Denise Akey, Gale Research Company, Detroit, MI.
   Vol. 1. *National Organizations of the United States*
   Vol. 2. *Geographic Index of National Organizations of the United States*
   Vol. 3. *Periodical Supplement of New Associations and Projects*

2. *Director of Consumer Protection and Environmental Agencies,*
Thaddeus C. Trzyna and the Staff of the Center for California Public
Affairs, and the Staff of Academic Media, Academic Media, Orange,
NJ.

(Example of the type of information included: "Select Committee
on Nutrition and Human Needs, 301 Senate Annex, Washington,
D.C. 20510, phone 202-225-7326. Conducts investigations into
hunger and poverty, and develops legislation to deal with those
problems.")

3. *Fine Arts Market Place,* edited by Paul Cummings, Archives of
American Art/Smithsonian Institution, published by R.R. Bowker
Co., New York and London.

4. *People's Yellow Pages of America,* edited by Richard Heller.
Richard Heller and Son, New Rochelle, NY.

When you go to the library to look for information you require, do
not hesitate to ask your librarian for help. The librarian is a well-
informed individual, capable of giving you sound advice on the
books you should consult in the reference department.

Art groups can get information through one of the following
agencies:

1. **Bay Area Lawyers for the Arts**
   25 Taylor St.
   San Francisco, CA 94102
2. **Lawyers for the Creative Arts**
   111 North Wabash Ave.
   Chicago, IL 60602
3. **Volunteer Lawyers for the Arts**
   36 West 44th St.
   New York, NY 10036
4. **National Endowment for the Arts.** For their free guides to programs write to: Public Information Officer, National Endowment
   for the Arts, Washington, D.C. 20506

Some other agencies that might be of help are:

1. **National Association of Investment Clubs**
   1515 East Eleven Mile Road
   Royal Oak, MI 48068
   (For information on forming investment clubs.)
2. **Citizen Action Group**
   133 C Street, S.E.
   Washington, D.C. 20036
   (Helps consumer groups to organize.)
3. **National Science Foundation**
   Public Affairs Office
   Washington, D.C. 20550
   (For guide to programs on funding for research and educational
   projects.)

Information on problems of senior citizens can be obtained from:

1. **National Council on the Aging, Inc.**
   200 Park Ave. South
   New York, NY 10010
2. **President's Council on Aging**
   Health, Education and Welfare Building
   Washington, D.C. 20201

Acknowledgments

The authors wish to thank the organizations to which they have belonged for the experience gained which enabled them to write this book. We are grateful to Marguerite Brewster, Joy Douglas, Sharlya Gold, Margaret Haun, and Lewis Moore for help and advice and to Patricia Lieb and Carol Schott for permission to use *Pteranodon's* poetry contest rules.

Information about tax exemption was taken directly, with permission, from Internal Revenue Service Publication 557, *How To Apply for and Retain Exempt Status for your Organization,* and from the "Application for Recognition of Exemption, under Section 501 (c) (3) of the Internal Revenue Code," Form 1023 and instructions Form 872-C. Other pamphlets referred to are *Instructions for Form 990-T, Circular E and Supplement, Employer's Tax Guide, Instructions for Schedule A (Form 990)* and Publication 526, *Income Tax Deductions for Contributions.*

Index